Dwight P. Berry

Vitamins
for the
Soul

A Topical Digest of Scripture Verses
for Inspiration and Instruction

TATE PUBLISHING & *Enterprises*

Published by Tate Publishing & Enterprises, LLC
127 E. Trade Center Terrace | Mustang, Oklahoma 73064 USA
1.888.361.9473 | www.tatepublishing.com

Tate Publishing is committed to excellence in the publishing industry. The company reflects the philosophy established by the founders, based on Psalm 68:11,
"The Lord gave the word and great was the company of those who published it."

Book design copyright © 2007 by Tate Publishing, LLC. All rights reserved.
Cover design by Jacob Crissup
Interior design by Leah LeFlore

Published in the United States of America

ISBN: 978-1-60247-554-0
1. Bible Study   2. Reference: Handbook
07.09.27

Dedication

In memory of

Louise Davis Berry

who first taught me the power
and inspiration of the Scriptures.

Acknowledgments

Gratitude and appreciation are expressed to

Laura Avery, Jason Batten, Bill
Erwin, and Wayne Williams

for their encouragement and tireless
efforts assisting me with the editing pro-
cess in bringing this book to fruition.

Contents

Introduction

With 66 books, 1,189 chapters, and nearly 774,000 words, the Bible can be intimidating. The inspiration for compiling *Vitamins for the Soul* was to lessen the intimidation factor by assembling a digest of key Scripture verses on timely topics, organized in a user-friendly format. Locating Scriptures that will provide strength, courage, inspiration, and instruction for a particular need can be a daunting task. With the realization that, short of an exhaustive topical Bible, no compilation of Scriptures can be all-inclusive, the most arduous task was determining which verses to omit.

The 155 topics included in *Vitamins for the Soul* are arranged alphabetically. The 1,675 verses are organized chronologically in book-chapter-verse order under each of the topical headings. Scripture passages were selected from four translations: New International Version, New American Standard Bible, New King James Version, and the Amplified Bible.

Readers are encouraged to browse the Table of Contents to familiarize themselves with the broad range of included topics. Verse identifications and translation abbreviations are included after each passage in the hope that readers might be inspired to read the provided passages in context.

Addiction

Wine is a mocker, strong drink a brawler, and whoever is intoxicated by it is not wise.

(Proverbs 20:1, NASB)

Do not be with heavy drinkers of wine, or with gluttonous eaters of meat; for the heavy drinker and the glutton will come to poverty, and drowsiness will clothe one with rags.

(Proverbs 23:20–21, NASB)

Who has woe? Who has sorrow? Who has strife? Who has complaints? Who has needless bruises? Who has bloodshot eyes? Those who linger over wine, who go to sample bowls of mixed wine. In the end it bites like a snake and poisons like a viper. Your eyes will see strange sights and your mind imagine confusing things. You will be like one sleeping on the high seas, lying on top of the rigging. "They hit me," you will say, "but I'm not hurt! They beat me, but I don't feel it! When will I wake up so I can find another drink?"

(Proverbs 23:29–30; 32–35, NIV)

Let us behave decently, as in the daytime, not in orgies and drunkenness, not in sexual immorality and debauchery, not in dissension and jealousy. Rather, clothe yourselves with the Lord Jesus Christ, and do not think about how to gratify the desires of the sinful nature.

(Romans 13:13–14, NIV)

All things are lawful for me, but not all things are profitable. All things are lawful for me, but I will not be mastered by anything.

(1 Corinthians 6:12, NASB)

Do you not know that your body is a temple of the Holy Spirit, who is in you, whom you have received from God? You are not your own; you were bought at a price. Therefore honor God with your body.

(1 Corinthians 6:19–20, NIV)

No temptation has seized you except what is common to man. And God is faithful; he will not let you be tempted beyond what you can bear. But when you are tempted, he will also provide a way out so that you can stand up under it.

(1 Corinthians 10:13, NIV)

And do not get drunk with wine, for that is debauchery; but ever be filled and stimulated with the [Holy] Spirit.

(Ephesians 5:18, AMP)

Submit yourselves, then, to God. Resist the devil, and he will flee from you.

(James 4:7, NIV)

For we have spent enough of our past lifetime in doing the will of the Gentiles—when we walked in lewdness, lusts, drunkenness, revelries, drinking parties, and abominable idolatries.

(1 Peter 4:3, NKJV)

For by whatever anyone is made inferior or worse or is overcome, to that [person or thing] he is enslaved.

(2 Peter 2:19b, AMP)

Affection (Brotherly Love)

Love must be sincere. Hate what is evil; cling to what is good. Be devoted to one another in brotherly love. Honor one another above yourselves.

(Romans 12:9–10, NIV)

Now as to the love of the brethren, you have no need for anyone to write to you, for you yourselves are taught by God to love one another.

(1 Thessalonians 4:9, NASB)

To sum up, all of you be harmonious, sympathetic, brotherly, kindhearted, and humble in spirit.

(1 Peter 3:8, NASB)

Above all things have intense and unfailing love for one another, for love covers a multitude of sins [forgives and disregards the offenses of others].

(1 Peter 4:8, AMP)

Whoever loves his brother lives in the light, and there is nothing in him to make him stumble.

(1 John 2:10, NIV)

Dear children, let us not love with words or tongue but with actions and in truth.

(1 John 3:18, NIV)

Dear friends, let us love one another, for love comes from God. Everyone who loves has been born of God and knows God. Whoever does not love does not know God, because God is love.

(1 John 4:7–8, NIV)

Beloved, if God so loved us, we also ought to love one another.

(1 John 4:11, NKJV)

Affliction
(see Hardship and Sickness)

Aging

Wisdom is with aged men, and with length of days, understanding.

(Job 12:12, NKJV)

"I thought age should speak, and increased years should teach wisdom. But it is a spirit in man, and the breath of the Almighty gives them understanding."

(Job 32:7–8, NASB)

Lord, make me to know my end and [to appreciate] the measure of my days—what it is; let me know and realize how frail I am [how transient is my stay here]. Behold, You have made my days as [short as] handbreadths, and my lifetime is as nothing in Your sight. Truly every man at his best is merely a breath! And now, Lord, what do I wait for and expect? My hope and expectation are in You.

(Psalm 39:4–5; 7, AMP)

Cast me not off nor send me away in the time of old age; forsake me not when my strength is spent and my powers fail.

(Psalm 71:9, AMP)

O God, You have taught me from my youth; and to this day I declare Your wondrous works. Now also when I am old and grayheaded, O God, do not forsake me, until I declare Your strength to this generation, Your power to everyone who is to come.

(Psalm 71:17–18, NKJV)

My flesh and my heart fail; but God is the strength of my heart and my portion forever.

(Psalm 73:26, NKJV)

The length of our days is seventy years—or eighty, if we have the strength; yet their span is but trouble and sorrow, for they quickly pass, and we fly away. Teach us to number our days aright, that we may gain a heart of wisdom.

(Psalm 90:10, 12, NIV)

For my days have been consumed in smoke. And my bones have been scorched like a hearth. My heart has been smitten like grass and has withered away. Indeed, I forget to eat my bread. Because of the loudness of my groaning my bones cling to my flesh. He has regarded the prayer of the destitute and has not despised their prayer.

(Psalm 102:3–5; 17, NASB)

Bless the Lord, O my soul, and forget not all His benefits: Who satisfies your mouth with good things, so that your youth is renewed like the eagle's.

(Psalm 103:2, 5, NKJV)

My son, do not forget my teaching, but let your heart keep my commandments; for length of days and years of life and peace they will add to you.

(Proverbs 3:1–2, NASB)

A gray head is a crown of glory; it is found in the way of righteousness.

(Proverbs 16:31, NASB)

The glory of young men is their strength, and the splendor of old men is their gray head.

(Proverbs 20:29, NKJV)

Do not say, Why were the old days better than these? For it is not wise or because of wisdom that you ask this.

(Ecclesiastes 7:10, AMP)

Even to your old age and gray hairs I am he, I am he who will sustain you.

(Isaiah 46:4a, NIV)

When I was a child, I spoke as a child, I understood as a child, I thought as a child; but when I became a man, I put away childish things.

(1 Corinthians 13:11, NKJV)

Therefore we do not lose heart, but though our outer man is decaying, yet our inner man is being renewed day by day. For momentary, light affliction is producing for us an eternal weight of glory far beyond all comparison, while we look not at the things which are seen, but at the things which are not seen; for the things which are seen are temporal, but the things which are not seen are eternal.

(2 Corinthians 4:16–18, NASB)

Do not rebuke an older man harshly, but exhort him as if he were your father. Treat younger men as brothers, older women as mothers, and younger women as sisters, with absolute purity.

(1 Timothy 5:1–2, NIV)

But as for you, speak the things which are fitting for sound doctrine. Older men are to be temperate, dignified, sensible, sound in faith, in love, in perseverance. Older women likewise are to be reverent in their behavior, not malicious gossips nor enslaved to much wine, teaching what is good, so that they may encourage the young women to love their husbands, to love their children, to be sensible, pure, workers at home, kind, being subject to their own husbands, so that the word of God will not be dishonored.

(Titus 2:1–5, NASB)

Alcoholism
(see Addiction)

Anger
(see also Speech, Careless)

Cease from anger and forsake wrath; fret not yourself—it tends only to evildoing.

(Psalm 37:8, AMP)

A quick-tempered man acts foolishly, and a man of evil devices is hated.

(Proverbs 14:17, NASB)

A soft answer turns away wrath, but a harsh word stirs up anger.

(Proverbs 15:1, NKJV)

A hot-tempered man stirs up strife, but the slow to anger calms a dispute.

(Proverbs 15:18, NASB)

He who is slow to anger is better than the mighty, he who rules his [own] spirit than he who takes a city.

(Proverbs 16:32, AMP)

A man of great wrath shall suffer the penalty; for if you deliver him [from the consequences], he will [feel free to] cause you to do it again.

(Proverbs 19:19, Amp)

Make no friendships with a man given to anger, and with a wrathful man do not associate, lest you learn his ways and get yourself into a snare.

(Proverbs 22:24–25, Amp)

Do you see a man who is hasty in his words? There is more hope for a [self-confident] fool than for him. A man of wrath stirs up strife, and a man given to anger commits and causes much transgression.

(Proverbs 29:20, 22, Amp)

Do not be eager in your heart to be angry, for anger resides in the bosom of fools.

(Ecclesiastes 7:9, nasb)

You have heard that it was said to the people long ago, "Do not murder, and anyone who murders will be subject to judgment. But I tell you that anyone who is angry with his brother will be subject to judgment.

(Matthew 5:21–22a, niv)

Be angry, and yet do not sin; do not let the sun go down on your anger.

(Ephesians 4:26, nasb)

Let all bitterness and wrath and anger and clamor and slander be put away from you, along with all malice.

(Ephesians 4:31, NASB)

Understand [this], my beloved brethren. Let every man be quick to hear [a ready listener], slow to speak, slow to take offense and to get angry. For man's anger does not promote the righteousness God [wishes and requires].

(James 1:19–20, AMP)

Arguing

The beginning of strife is as when water first trickles [from a crack in a dam]; therefore stop contention before it becomes worse and quarreling breaks out.

(Proverbs 17:14, AMP)

He who loves a quarrel loves sin.

(Proverbs 17:19a, NIV)

You are still worldly. For since there is jealousy and quarreling among you, are you not worldly? Are you not acting like mere men?

(1 Corinthians 3:3, NIV)

Do everything without complaining or arguing.

(Philippians 2:14, NIV)

But refuse (shut your mind against, have nothing to do with) trifling (ill-informed, unedifying, stupid) controversies over ignorant questionings, for you know that they foster strife and breed quarrels. And the servant of the Lord must not be quarrelsome (fighting and contending). Instead, he must be kindly to everyone and mild-tempered [preserving the bond of peace]; he must be a skilled and suitable teacher, patient and forbearing and willing to suffer wrong.

(2 Timothy 2:23–24, AMP)

Arrogance
(see also Conceit and Pride)

Talk no more so very proudly; let no arrogance come from your mouth, for the Lord is the God of knowledge; and by Him actions are weighed.

(1 Samuel 2:3, NKJV)

He does not answer when men cry out because of the arrogance of the wicked. Indeed, God does not listen to their empty plea; the Almighty pays no attention to it.

(Job 35:12–13, NIV)

The fear of the Lord is to hate evil; pride and arrogance and the evil way and the perverted mouth, I hate.

(Proverbs 8:13, NASB)

A [self-confident] fool has no delight in understanding but only in revealing his personal opinions and himself.

(Proverbs 18:2, AMP)

Haughtiness comes before disaster, but humility before honor.

(Proverbs 18:12, Amp)

Let another man praise you, and not your own mouth; a stranger, and not your own lips.

(Proverbs 27:2, Amp)

Thus I will punish the world for its evil and the wicked for their iniquity; I will also put an end to the arrogance of the proud and abase the haughtiness of the ruthless.

(Isaiah 13:11, nasb)

But this is not to be so among you; instead, whoever desires to be great among you must be your servant, and whoever wishes to be most important and first in rank among you must be slave of all. For even the Son of Man came not to have service rendered to Him, but to serve, and to give His life as a ransom for (instead of) many.

(Mark 10:43–45, Amp)

For everyone who exalts himself will be humbled, and he who humbles himself will be exalted.

(Luke 14:11, nasb)

Also He spoke this parable to some who trusted in them-selves that they were righteous, and despised others: "Two men went up to the temple to pray, one a Pharisee and the other a tax collector. The Pharisee stood and prayed thus with himself, 'God, I thank You that I am not like other men—extortioners, unjust, adulterers, or even as this tax collector. I fast twice a week; I give tithes of all that I possess.' "And the tax collector, standing afar off, would not so much as raise his eyes to heaven, but beat his breast, saying, 'God, be merciful to me a sinner!' "I tell you, this man went down to his house justified rather than the other; for everyone who exalts himself will be humbled, and he who humbles himself will be exalted."

(Luke 18:9–14, NKJV)

So, if you think you are standing firm, be careful that you don't fall!

(1 Corinthians 10:12, NIV)

For we are not bold to class or compare ourselves with some of those who commend themselves; but when they measure themselves by themselves and compare themselves with themselves, they are without understanding.

(2 Corinthians 10:12, NASB)

Astrology
(see Superstition)

Atheism

In His hand is the life of every living thing and the breath of all mankind.

(Job 12:10, AMP)

The fool has said in his heart, "There is no God."

(Psalm 53:1a, NKJV)

For since the creation of the world His invisible attributes, His eternal power and divine nature, have been clearly seen, being understood through what has been made, so that they are without excuse. For even though they knew God, they did not honor Him as God or give thanks, but they became futile in their speculations, and their foolish heart was darkened.

(Romans 1:20–21, NASB)

Backsliding

The mouth of the [uncompromisingly] righteous utters wisdom, and his tongue speaks with justice. The law of his God is in his heart; none of his steps shall slide.

(Psalm 37:30–31, AMP)

Let your eyes look directly ahead and let your gaze be fixed straight in front of you. Watch the path of your feet and all your ways will be established. Do not turn to the right nor to the left; turn your foot from evil.

(Proverbs 4:25–27, NASB)

Let the wicked forsake his way, and the unrighteous man his thoughts; let him return to the Lord, and He will have mercy on him; and to our God, for He will abundantly pardon.

(Isaiah 55:7, NKJV)

Return, you backsliding children, and I will heal your backslidings.

(Jeremiah 3:22a, NKJV)

Let us examine our ways and test them, and let us return to the Lord.

(Lamentations 3:40, NIV)

You are the salt of the earth; but if the salt has become tasteless, how can it be made salty again? It is no longer good for anything, except to be thrown out and trampled under foot by men.

(Matthew 5:13, NASB)

But Jesus said to him, "No one, having put his hand to the plow, and looking back, is fit for the kingdom of God."

(Luke 9:62, NKJV)

If a person does not dwell in Me, he is thrown out like a [broken-off] branch, and withers; such branches are gathered up and thrown into the fire, and they are burned.

(John 15:6, AMP)

So, if you think you are standing firm, be careful that you don't fall! No temptation has seized you except what is common to man. And God is faithful; he will not let you be tempted beyond what you can bear. But when you are tempted, he will also provide a way out so that you can stand up under it.

(1 Corinthians 10:12–13, NIV)

But now that you know God—or rather are known by God—how is it that you are turning back to those weak and miserable principles? Do you wish to be enslaved by them all over again?

(Galatians 4:9, NIV)

Avoiding worldly and empty chatter and the opposing arguments of what is falsely called "knowledge"—which some have professed and thus gone astray from the faith.

(1 Timothy 6:20b-21a, NASB)

See to it, brothers, that none of you has a sinful, unbelieving heart that turns away from the living God.

(Hebrews 3:12, NIV)

So let us seize and hold fast and retain without wavering the hope we cherish and confess and our acknowledgement of it, for He Who promised is reliable (sure) and faithful to His word. For if we go on deliberately and willingly sinning after once acquiring the knowledge of the Truth, there is no longer any sacrifice left to atone for [our] sins [no further offering to which to look forward]. [There is nothing left for us then] but a kind of awful and fearful prospect and expectation of divine judgment and the fury of burning wrath and indignation which will consume those who put themselves in opposition [to God].

(Hebrews 10:23; 26–27, AMP)

But my righteous one will live by faith. And if he shrinks back, I will not be pleased with him.

(Hebrews 10:38, NIV)

My brethren, if any among you strays from the truth and one turns him back, let him know that he who turns a sinner from the error of his way will save his soul from death and will cover a multitude of sins.

(James 5:19–20, NASB)

You therefore, beloved, knowing this beforehand, be on your guard so that you are not carried away by the error of unprincipled men and fall from your own steadfastness.

(2 Peter 3:17, NASB)

Believing
(see also Repentance and Salvation)

All things are possible to him who believes.

(Mark 9:23b, NASB)

He who believes and is baptized will be saved; but he who does not believe will be condemned.

(Mark 16:16, NKJV)

He who believes in Him is not judged; he who does not believe has been judged already, because he has not believed in the name of the only begotten Son of God.

(John 3:18, NASB)

Whoever believes in the Son has eternal life, but whoever rejects the Son will not see life, for God's wrath remains on him.

(John 3:36, NIV)

Then He said to Thomas, "Reach here with your finger,

and see My hands; and reach here your hand and put it into My side; and do not be unbelieving, but believing."

Thomas answered and said to Him, "My Lord and my God!"

Jesus said to him, "Because you have seen Me, have you believed? Blessed are they who did not see, and yet believed."

(John 20:27–29, NASB)

For the Scripture says, "Whoever believes in Him will not be disappointed."

(Romans 10:11, NASB)

Burdens, Bearing One Another's
(see also Compassion)

Now we who are strong ought to bear the weaknesses of those without strength and not just please ourselves.

(Romans 15:1, NASB)

For it has been the good pleasure of Macedonia and Achaia to make some contribution for the poor among the saints of Jerusalem.

(Romans 15:26, AMP)

Bear one another's burdens, and so fulfill the law of Christ.

(Galatians 6:2, NKJV)

Therefore encourage one another and build each other up, just as in fact you are doing. And we urge you, brothers, warn those who are idle, encourage the timid, help the weak, be patient with everyone.

(1 Thessalonians 5:11, 14, NIV)

Business
(see also Working)

This Book of the Law shall not depart out of your mouth, but you shall meditate on it day and night, that you may observe and do according to all that is written in it. For then you shall make your way prosperous, and then you shall deal wisely and have good success.

(Joshua 1:8, AMP)

If they obey and serve Him, they shall spend their days in prosperity, and their years in pleasures.

(Job 36:11, NKJV)

Blessed is the man who walks not in the counsel of the ungodly, nor stands in the path of sinners, nor sits in the seat of the scornful; but his delight is in the law of the Lord, and in His law he meditates day and night. He shall be like a tree planted by the rivers of water, that brings forth its fruit in its season, whose leaf also shall not wither; and whatever he does shall prosper.

(Psalm 1:1–3, NKJV)

No good thing will He withhold from those who walk uprightly.

(Psalm 84:11c, AMP)

It is well with the man who deals generously and lends, who conducts his affairs with justice.

(Psalm 112:5, AMP)

Commit to the Lord whatever you do, and your plans will succeed.

(Proverbs 16:3, NIV)

The plans of the diligent lead surely to advantage, but everyone who is hasty comes surely to poverty.

(Proverbs 21:5, NASB)

Character
(see also Righteousness and Witnessing)

Let the words of my mouth and the meditation of my heart be acceptable in Your sight, O Lord, my strength and my Redeemer.

(Psalm 19:14, NKJV)

You who love the Lord, hate evil! He preserves the souls of His saints; He delivers them out of the hand of the wicked.

(Psalm 97:10, NKJV)

How blessed are those whose way is blameless, who walk in the law of the Lord.

(Psalm 119:1, NASB)

Do not withhold good from those to whom it is due, when it is in your power to do it. Do not say to your neighbor, "Go, and come back, and tomorrow I will give it," when you have it with you.

(Proverbs 3:27–28, NASB)

So in everything, do to others what you would have them do to you, for this sums up the Law and the Prophets.

(Matthew 7:12, NIV)

Salt is good; but if the salt becomes unsalty, with what will you make it salty again? Have salt in yourselves, and be at peace with one another.

(Mark 9:50, NASB)

Jesus answered and said to him, "Most assuredly, I say to you, unless one is born again, he cannot see the kingdom of God."

(John 3:3, NKJV)

If anyone serves Me, he must follow Me; and where I am, there My servant will be also; if anyone serves Me, the Father will honor him.

(John 12:26, NASB)

I give you a new commandment: that you should love one another, just as I have loved you, so you too should love one another. By this shall all [men] know that you are My disciples, if you love one another [if you keep on showing love among yourselves.]

(John 13:34–35, AMP)

If you love Me, you will keep My commandments.

(John 14:15, NASB)

Jesus answered and said to him, "If anyone loves Me, he will keep My word; and My Father will love him, and We will come to him and make Our abode with him.

(John 14:23, NASB)

Therefore, I urge you, brothers, in view of God's mercy, to offer your bodies as living sacrifices, holy and pleasing to God—this is your spiritual act of worship. Do not conform any longer to the pattern of this world, but be transformed by the renewing of your mind. Then you will be able to test and approve what God's will is—his good, pleasing and perfect will.

(Romans 12:1–2, NIV)

Let us behave decently, as in the daytime, not in orgies and drunkenness, not in sexual immorality and debauchery, not in dissension and jealousy. Rather, clothe yourselves with the Lord Jesus Christ, and do not think about how to gratify the desires of the sinful nature.

(Romans 13:13–14, NIV)

I urge you, brothers, to watch out for those who cause divisions and put obstacles in your way that are contrary to the teaching you have learned. Keep away from them. For such people are not serving our Lord Christ, but their own appetites. By smooth talk and flattery they deceive the minds of naive people.

(Romans 16:17–18, NIV)

Do you not know that you are the temple of God and that the Spirit of God dwells in you? If anyone defiles the temple of God, God will destroy him. For the temple of God is holy, which temple you are.

(1 Corinthians 3:16–17, NKJV)

For as often as you eat this bread and drink this cup, you proclaim the Lord's death till He comes.

(1 Corinthians 11:26, NKJV)

Do not be deceived: "Bad company corrupts good morals."

(1 Corinthians 15:33, NASB)

Therefore, having these promises, beloved, let us cleanse ourselves from all defilement of flesh and spirit, perfecting holiness in the fear of God.

(2 Corinthians 7:1, NASB)

We demolish arguments and every pretension that sets itself up against the knowledge of God, and we take captive every thought to make it obedient to Christ.

(2 Corinthians 10:5, NIV)

But the fruit of the [Holy] Spirit [the work which His presence within accomplishes] is love, joy (gladness), peace, patience (an even temper, forbearance), kindness, goodness (benevolence), faithfulness, gentleness (meekness, humility), self-control (self-restraint, continence). Against such things there is no law [that can bring a charge].

(Galatians 5:22–23, AMP)

Let us not become conceited, provoking one another, envying one another.

(Galatians 5:26, NKJV)

Let us not become weary in doing good, for at the proper time we will reap a harvest if we do not give up. Therefore, as we have opportunity, let us do good to all people, especially to those who belong to the family of believers.

(Galatians 6:9–10, NIV)

As a result, we are no longer to be children, tossed here and there by waves and carried about by every wind of doctrine, by the trickery of men, by craftiness in deceitful scheming; but speaking the truth in love, we are to grow up in all aspects into Him who is the head, even Christ.

(Ephesians 4:14–15, NASB)

Be kind and compassionate to one another, forgiving each other, just as in Christ God forgave you.

(Ephesians 4:32, NIV)

Therefore be imitators of God [copy Him and follow His example], as well-beloved children [imitate their father]. But immorality (sexual vice) and all impurity [of lustful, rich, wasteful living] or greediness must not even be named among you, as is fitting and proper among saints (God's consecrated people). Let there be no filthiness (obscenity, indecency) nor foolish and sinful (silly and corrupt) talk, nor coarse jesting, which are not fitting or becoming; but instead voice your thankfulness [to God].

(Ephesians 5:1; 3–4, Amp)

Therefore take up the whole armor of God, that you may be able to withstand in the evil day, and having done all, to stand. Stand therefore, having girded your waist with truth, having put on the breastplate of righteousness, and having shod your feet with the preparation of the gospel of peace; above all, taking the shield of faith with which you will be able to quench all the fiery darts of the wicked one. And take the helmet of salvation, and the sword of the Spirit, which is the word of God.

(Ephesians 6:13–17, NKJV)

So that you will walk in a manner worthy of the Lord, to please Him in all respects, bearing fruit in every good work and increasing in the knowledge of God.

(Colossians 1:10, NASB)

Therefore if you have been raised up with Christ, keep seeking the things above, where Christ is, seated at the right hand of God. Set your mind on the things above, not on the things that are on earth. Therefore consider the members of your earthly body as dead to immorality, impurity, passion, evil desire, and greed, which amounts to idolatry. And in them you also once walked, when you were living in them. But now you also, put them all aside: anger, wrath, malice, slander, and abusive speech from your mouth.

(Colossians 3:1–2; 5; 7–8, NASB)

So, as those who have been chosen of God, holy and beloved, put on a heart of compassion, kindness, humility, gentleness and patience; bearing with one another, and forgiving each other, whoever has a complaint against anyone; just as the Lord forgave you, so also should you.

(Colossians 3:12–13, NASB)

And may the Lord cause you to increase and abound in love for one another, and for all people, just as we also do for you; so that He may establish your hearts without blame in holiness before our God and Father at the coming of our Lord Jesus with all His saints.

(1 Thessalonians 3:12–13, NASB)

For God did not call us to uncleanness, but in holiness. Therefore he who rejects this does not reject man, but God, who has also given us His Holy Spirit.

(1 Thessalonians 4:7–8, NKJV)

Test all things; hold fast what is good. Abstain from every form of evil.

(1 Thessalonians 5:21–22, NKJV)

But as for you, brethren, do not grow weary in doing good.

(2 Thessalonians 3:13, NKJV)

But you, O man of God, flee these things and pursue righteousness, godliness, faith, love, patience, gentleness. Fight the good fight of faith, lay hold on eternal life, to which you were also called and have confessed the good confession in the presence of many witnesses.

(1 Timothy 6:11–12, NKJV)

Nevertheless, God's solid foundation stands firm, sealed with this inscription: "The Lord knows those who are his," and, "Everyone who confesses the name of the Lord must turn away from wickedness."

(2 Timothy 2:19, NIV)

Our people must learn to devote themselves to doing what is good, in order that they may provide for daily necessities and not live unproductive lives.

(Titus 3:14, NIV)

Let us not give up meeting together, as some are in the habit of doing, but let us encourage one another—and all the more as you see the Day approaching.

(Hebrews 10:25, NIV)

But be doers of the word, and not hearers only, deceiving yourselves.

(James 1:22, NKJV)

Pure and undefiled religion in the sight of our God and Father is this: to visit orphans and widows in their distress, and to keep oneself unstained by the world.

(James 1:27, NASB)

Not returning evil for evil or reviling for reviling, but on the contrary blessing, knowing that you were called to this, that you may inherit a blessing. For "He who would love life and see good days, let him refrain his tongue from evil, and his lips from speaking deceit. Let him turn away from evil and do good; let him seek peace and pursue it. For the eyes of the Lord are on the righteous, and His ears are open to their prayers; but the face of the Lord is against those who do evil."

(1 Peter 3:9–12, NKJV)

Now for this very reason also, applying all diligence, in your faith supply moral excellence, and in your moral excellence, knowledge, and in your knowledge, self-control, and in your self-control, perseverance, and in your perseverance, godliness, and in your godliness, brotherly kindness, and in your brotherly kindness, love. For if these qualities are yours and are increasing, they render you neither useless nor unfruitful in the true knowledge of our Lord Jesus Christ. For he who lacks these qualities is blind or shortsighted, having forgotten his purification from his former sins.

(2 Peter 1:5–9, NASB)

If we confess our sins, he is faithful and just and will forgive us our sins and purify us from all unrighteousness.

(1 John 1:9, NIV)

By this we know that we are in Him. He who says he abides in Him ought himself also to walk just as He walked.

(1 John 2:5b-6, NKJV)

Church and State

Blessed is the nation whose God is the Lord.

(Psalm 33:12a, NKJV)

Shall the throne of iniquity have fellowship with You—they who frame and hide their unrighteous doings under [the sacred name of] law? They band themselves together against the life of the [consistently] righteous and condemn the innocent to death. But the Lord has become my High Tower and Defense, and my God the Rock of my refuge. And He will turn back upon them their own iniquity and will wipe them out by means of their own wickedness; the Lord our God will wipe them out.

(Psalm 94:20–23, AMP)

Pay therefore to Caesar the things that are due to Caesar, and pay to God the things that are due to God.

(Matthew 22:21b, AMP)

Every person is to be in subjection to the governing authorities. For there is no authority except from God, and those which exist are established by God. Therefore whoever resists authority has opposed the ordinance of God; and they who have opposed will receive condemnation upon themselves. Therefore it is necessary to be in subjection, not only because of wrath, but also for conscience' sake. For because of this you also pay taxes, for rulers are servants of God, devoting themselves to this very thing. Render to all what is due them: tax to whom tax is due; custom to whom custom; fear to whom fear; honor to whom honor.

(Romans 13:1–2, 5–7, NASB)

First of all, then, I admonish and urge that petitions, prayers, intercessions, and thanksgivings be offered on behalf of all men, for kings and all who are in positions of authority or high responsibility, that [outwardly] we may pass a quiet and undisturbed life [and inwardly] a peaceable one in all godliness and reverence and seriousness in every way.

(1 Timothy 2:1–2, AMP)

Remind them to be subject to rulers and authorities, to obey, to be ready for every good work, to speak evil of no one, to be peaceable, gentle, showing all humility to all men.

(Titus 3:1–2, NKJV)

Submit yourselves for the Lord's sake to every human institution, whether to a king as the one in authority, or to governors as sent by him for the punishment of evildoers and the praise of those who do right. For such is the will of God that by doing right you may silence the ignorance of foolish men. Act as free men, and do not use your freedom as a covering for evil, but use it as bondslaves of God. Honor all people, love the brotherhood, fear God, honor the king.

(1 Peter 2:13–17, NASB)

Comfort in Trouble
(see also Discouragement)

Even though I walk through the valley of the shadow of death, I will fear no evil, for you are with me; your rod and your staff, they comfort me.

(Psalm 23:4, NIV)

Guard my soul and deliver me; do not let me be ashamed, for I take refuge in You. Let integrity and uprightness preserve me, for I wait for You.

(Psalm 25:20–21, NASB)

The Lord is my strength and my shield; my heart trusted in Him, and I am helped.

(Psalm 28:7a, NKJV)

The lions may grow weak and hungry, but those who seek the Lord lack no good thing. The eyes of the Lord are on the righteous and his ears are attentive to their cry. A righteous man may have many troubles, but the Lord delivers him from them all.

(Psalm 34:10, 15, 19, NIV)

God is our refuge and strength, a very present help in trouble. Therefore we will not fear, even though the earth be removed, and though the mountains be carried into the midst of the sea; though its waters roar and be troubled, though the mountains shake with its swelling.

(Psalm 46:1–3, NKJV)

Cast your cares on the Lord and he will sustain you; he will never let the righteous fall.

(Psalm 55:22, NIV)

When anxiety was great within me, your consolation brought joy to my soul.

(Psalm 94:19, NIV)

This is my comfort and consolation in my affliction: that Your word has revived me and given me life. When I have [earnestly] recalled Your ordinances from of old, O Lord, I have taken comfort.

(Psalm 119:50, 52, AMP)

I will lift up my eyes to the hills—from whence comes my help? My help comes from the Lord, who made heaven and earth.

(Psalm 121:1–2, NKJV)

Save my life, O Lord, for Your name's sake; in Your righteousness, bring my life out of trouble and free me from distress.

(Psalm 143:11, AMP)

For the turning away of the simple will slay them, and the complacency of fools will destroy them; but whoever listens to me will dwell safely, and will be secure, without fear of evil.

(Proverbs 1:32–33, NKJV)

For I, the Lord your God, will hold your right hand, say-ing to you, "Fear not, I will help you."

(Isaiah 41:13, NKJV)

For the Lord will not reject forever, for if He causes grief, then He will have compassion according to His abundant lovingkindness. For He does not afflict willingly or grieve the sons of men.

(Lamentations 3:31–33, NASB)

The Lord is good, a stronghold in the day of trouble; and He knows those who trust in Him.

(Nahum 1:7, NKJV)

Come to me, all you who are weary and burdened, and I will give you rest.

(Matthew 11:28, NIV)

Jesus answered them, I assure you, most solemnly I tell you, whoever commits and practices sin is the slave of sin. So if the Son liberates you [makes you free men], then you are really and unquestionably free.

(John 8:34, 36, AMP)

There is therefore now no condemnation to those who are in Christ Jesus, who do not walk according to the flesh, but according to the Spirit. For the law of the Spirit of life in Christ Jesus has made me free from the law of sin and death.

(Romans 8:1–2, NKJV)

If God is for us, who can be against us? He who did not spare His own Son, but delivered Him up for us all, how shall He not with Him also freely give us all things?

(Romans 8:31b-32, NKJV)

However, as it is written: "No eye has seen, no ear has heard, no mind has conceived what God has prepared for those who love him."

(1 Corinthians 2:9, NIV)

Blessed be the God and Father of our Lord Jesus Christ, the Father of mercies and God of all comfort, who comforts us in all our affliction so that we will be able to comfort those who are in any affliction with the comfort with which we ourselves are comforted by God.

(2 Corinthians 1:3–4, NASB)

But the Lord is faithful, and He will strengthen and protect you from the evil one.

(2 Thessalonians 3:3, NASB)

Compassion

He answered and said to them, "He who has two tunics, let him give to him who has none; and he who has food, let him do likewise."

(Luke 3:11, NKJV)

Rejoice with those who rejoice; mourn with those who mourn.

(Romans 12:15, NIV)

But whoever has this world's goods, and sees his brother in need, and shuts up his heart from him, how does the love of God abide in him?

(1 John 3:17, NKJV)

Dear friends, let us love one another, for love comes from God. Everyone who loves has been born of God and knows God. Whoever does not love does not know God, because God is love. No one has ever seen God; but if we love one another, God lives in us and his love is made complete in us.

(1 John 4:7–8; 12, NIV)

Conceit
(see also Arrogance and Pride)

Trust in the Lord with all your heart and lean not on your own understanding.

(Proverbs 3:5, NIV)

The way of a fool is right in his own eyes, but he who heeds counsel is wise.

(Proverbs 12:15, NKJV)

Woe to those who are wise in their own eyes, and prudent in their own sight!

(Isaiah 5:21, NKJV)

Thus says the Lord: "Let not the wise man glory in his wisdom, let not the mighty man glory in his might, nor let the rich man glory in his riches."

(Jeremiah 9:23, NKJV)

For by the grace given me I say to every one of you: Do not think of yourself more highly than you ought, but rather think of yourself with sober judgment, in accordance with the measure of faith God has given you.

(Romans 12:3, NIV)

Live in harmony with one another. Do not be proud, but be willing to associate with people of low position. Do not be conceited.

(Romans 12:16, NIV)

If anyone thinks he is something when he is nothing, he deceives himself. Each one should test his own actions. Then he can take pride in himself, without comparing himself to somebody else, for each one should carry his own load.

(Galatians 6:3–5, NIV)

Do nothing out of selfish ambition or vain conceit, but in humility consider others better than yourselves. Each of you should look not only to your own interests, but also to the interests of others.

(Philippians 2:3–4, NIV)

But know this, that in the last days perilous times will come: for men will be lovers of themselves, lovers of money, boasters, proud, blasphemers, disobedient to parents, unthankful, unholy, unloving, unforgiving, slanderers, without self-control, brutal, despisers of good, traitors, headstrong, haughty, lovers of pleasure rather than lovers of God, having a form of godliness but denying its power. And from such people turn away!

(2 Timothy 3:1–5, NKJV)

Confidence

I have set the Lord always before me; because He is at my right hand I shall not be moved.

(Psalm 16:8, NKJV)

Now as for me, I said in my prosperity, "I will never be moved." O Lord, by Your favor You have made my mountain to stand strong; you hid Your face, I was dismayed. Hear, O Lord, and be gracious to me; O Lord, be my helper."

(Psalm 30:6–7, 10, NASB)

If the Lord delights in a man's way, he makes his steps firm; though he stumble, he will not fall, for the Lord upholds him with his hand.

(Psalm 37:23–24, NIV)

Do not be afraid of sudden terror, nor of trouble from the wicked when it comes; for the Lord will be your confidence, and will keep your foot from being caught.

(Proverbs 3:25–26, NKJV)

In the reverent and worshipful fear of the Lord there is strong confidence, and His children shall always have a place of refuge.

(Proverbs 14:26, Amp)

Therefore having such a hope, we use great boldness in our speech.

(2 Corinthians 3:12, nasb)

In him and through faith in him we may approach God with freedom and confidence.

(Ephesians 3:12, niv)

But one thing I do, forgetting those things which are behind and reaching forward to those things which are ahead, I press toward the goal for the prize of the upward call of God in Christ Jesus.

(Philippians 3:13b-14, nkjv)

I can do everything through him who gives me strength.

(Philippians 4:13, niv)

We have come to share in Christ if we hold firmly till the end the confidence we had at first.

(Hebrews 3:14, niv)

So do not throw away your confidence; it will be richly rewarded.

(Hebrews 10:35, niv)

So we may boldly say: "The Lord is my helper; I will not fear. What can man do to me?"

(Hebrews 13:6, NKJV)

And now, little children, abide in Him, that when He appears, we may have confidence and not be ashamed before Him at His coming.

(1 John 2:28, NKJV)

We have come to know and have believed the love which God has for us. God is love, and the one who abides in love abides in God, and God abides in him. By this, love is perfected with us, so that we may have confidence in the day of judgment; because as He is, so also are we in this world.

(1 John 4:16–17, NASB)

This is the confidence we have in approaching God: that if we ask anything according to his will, he hears us.

(1 John 5:14, NIV)

Conflict
(see Trouble)

Conscience

I will maintain my righteousness and never let go of it; my conscience will not reproach me as long as I live.

(Job 27:6, NIV)

In view of this, I also do my best to maintain always a blameless conscience both before God and before men.

(Acts 24:16, NASB)

My conscience is clear, but that does not make me innocent. It is the Lord who judges me. Therefore judge nothing before the appointed time; wait till the Lord comes. He will bring to light what is hidden in darkness and will expose the motives of men's hearts. At that time each will receive his praise from God.

(1 Corinthians 4:4–5, NIV)

For our proud confidence is this: the testimony of our conscience, that in holiness and godly sincerity, not in fleshly wisdom but in the grace of God, we have conducted ourselves in the world, and especially toward you.

(2 Corinthians 1:12, NASB)

Now the purpose of the commandment is love from a pure heart, from a good conscience, and from sincere faith.

(1 Timothy 1:5, NKJV)

To the pure [in heart and conscience] all things are pure, but to the defiled and corrupt and unbelieving nothing is pure; their very minds and consciences are defiled and polluted.

(Titus 1:15, AMP)

How much more, then, will the blood of Christ, who through the eternal Spirit offered himself unblemished to God, cleanse our consciences from acts that lead to death, so that we may serve the living God!

(Hebrews 9:14, NIV)

Let us draw near with a sincere heart in full assurance of faith, having our hearts sprinkled clean from an evil conscience and our bodies washed with pure water.

(Hebrews 10:22, NASB)

Keep praying for us, for we are convinced that we have a good (clear) conscience, that we want to walk uprightly and live a noble life, acting honorably and in complete honesty in all things.

(Hebrews 13:18, AMP)

Little children, let us not love with word or with tongue, but in deed and truth. We will know by this that we are of the truth, and will assure our heart before Him in whatever our heart condemns us; for God is greater than our heart and knows all things. Beloved, if our heart does not condemn us, we have confidence before God.

(1 John 3:18–21, NASB)

Contentment
(see also Peace, Inner)

The Lord is my chosen and assigned portion, my cup; You hold and maintain my lot. The lines have fallen for me in pleasant places; yes, I have a good heritage.

(Psalm 16:5–6, AMP)

All the days of the desponding and afflicted are made evil [by anxious thoughts and forebodings], but he who has a glad heart has a continual feast [regardless of circumstances].

(Proverbs 15:15, AMP)

Remove far from me falsehood and lies; give me neither poverty nor riches; feed me with the food that is needful for me, lest I be full and deny You and say, Who is the Lord? Or lest I be poor and steal, and so profane the name of my God.

(Proverbs 30:8–9, AMP)

Better a handful with quietness than both hands full, together with toil and grasping for the wind.

(Ecclesiastes 4:6, NKJV)

On the contrary, who are you, O man, who answers back to God? The thing molded will not say to the molder, "Why did you make me like this," will it? Or does not the potter have a right over the clay, to make from the same lump one vessel for honorable use and another for common use?

(Romans 9:20–21, NASB)

As sorrowful, yet always rejoicing; as poor, yet making many rich; as having nothing, and yet possessing all things.

(2 Corinthians 6:10, NKJV)

I know what it is to be in need, and I know what it is to have plenty. I have learned the secret of being content in any and every situation, whether well fed or hungry, whether living in plenty or in want. I can do everything through him who gives me strength.

(Philippians 4:12–13, NIV)

But godliness with contentment is great gain. For we brought nothing into the world, and we can take nothing out of it.

(1 Timothy 6:6–7, NIV)

Make sure that your character is free from the love of money, being content with what you have; for He Himself has said, "I will never desert you, nor will I ever forsake you."

(Hebrews 13:5, NASB)

Courage
(see Strength)

Criticism

When they kept on questioning him, he straightened up and said to them, "If any one of you is without sin, let him be the first to throw a stone at her."

(John 8:7, NIV)

For what credit is there if, when you sin and are harshly treated, you endure it with patience? But if when you do what is right and suffer for it you patiently endure it, this finds favor with God.

(1 Peter 2:20, NASB)

Death

(see also Eternal Life and Judgment and Paradise)

In the sweat of your face shall you eat bread until you return to the ground, for out of it you were taken; for dust you are and to dust you shall return.

(Genesis 3:19, AMP)

Since a man's days are already determined, and the number of his months is wholly in Your control, and he cannot pass the bounds of his allotted time.

(Job 14:5, AMP)

Even though I walk through the valley of the shadow of death, I will fear no evil, for you are with me; your rod and your staff, they comfort me.

(Psalm 23:4, NIV)

No man can by any means redeem his brother or give to God a ransom for him—for the redemption of his soul is costly, and he should cease trying forever—that he should live on eternally, that he should not undergo decay.

(Psalm 49:7–9, NASB)

What man can live and not see death? Can he deliver his life from the power of the grave?

(Psalm 89:48, NKJV)

Lord, you have been our dwelling place in all generations. Before the mountains were born or You gave birth to the earth and the world, even from everlasting to everlasting, You are God. You turn man back into dust and say, "Return, O children of men." For a thousand years in Your sight are like yesterday when it passes by, or as a watch in the night.

(Psalm 90:1–4, NASB)

As for man, his days are as grass; as a flower of the field, so he flourishes. For the wind passes over it and it is gone, and its place shall know it no more. But the mercy and loving-kindness of the Lord are from everlasting to everlasting upon those who reverently and worshipfully fear Him, and His righteousness is to children's children.

(Psalm 103:15–17a, AMP)

The cords and sorrows of death were around me, and the terrors of Sheol (the place of the dead) had laid hold of me; I suffered anguish and grief (trouble and sorrow). Then called I upon the name of the Lord: O Lord, I beseech You, save my life and deliver me! Gracious is the Lord, and [rigidly] righteous; yes, our God is merciful.

(Psalm 116:3–5, AMP)

Precious in the sight of the Lord is the death of His saints.

(Psalm 116:15, NKJV)

Reverent and worshipful fear of the Lord is a fountain of life, that one may avoid the snares of death. The wicked is overthrown through his wrongdoing and calamity, but the [consistently] righteous has hope and confidence even in death.

(Proverbs 14:27, 32, AMP)

Since no man knows the future, who can tell him what is to come? No man has power over the wind to contain it; so no one has power over the day of his death.

(Ecclesiastes 8:7–8a,b, NIV)

Then the dust will return to the earth as it was, and the spirit will return to God who gave it.

(Ecclesiastes 12:7, NKJV)

The righteous perish, and no one ponders it in his heart; devout men are taken away, and no one understands that the righteous are taken away to be spared from evil. Those who walk uprightly enter into peace; they find rest as they lie in death.

(Isaiah 57:1–2, NIV)

I tell you the truth, whoever hears my word and believes him who sent me has eternal life and will not be condemned; he has crossed over from death to life.

(John 5:24, NIV)

Jesus said to her, "I am the resurrection and the life. He who believes in Me, though he may die, he shall live. And whoever lives and believes in Me shall never die. Do you believe this?"

(John 11:25–26, NKJV)

And they stoned Stephen as he was calling on God and saying, "Lord Jesus, receive my spirit."

(Acts 7:59, NKJV)

For none of us lives to himself alone and none of us dies to himself alone. If we live, we live to the Lord; and if we die, we die to the Lord. So, whether we live or die, we belong to the Lord.

(Romans 14:7–8, NIV)

If we have hoped in Christ in this life only, we are of all men most to be pitied. But now Christ has been raised from the dead, the first fruits of those who are asleep. For since by a man came death, by a man also came the resurrection of the dead. For as in Adam all die, so also in Christ all will be made alive. The last enemy that will be abolished is death.

(1 Corinthians 15:19–22, 26, NASB)

Behold, I tell you a mystery: We shall not all sleep, but we shall all be changed—in a moment, in the twinkling of an eye, at the last trumpet. For the trumpet will sound, and the dead will be raised incorruptible, and we shall be changed. For this corruptible must put on incorruption, and this mortal must put on immortality. So when this corruptible has put on incorruption, and this mortal has put on immortality, then shall be brought to pass the saying that is written: "Death is swallowed up in victory. O Death, where is your sting? O Hades, where is your victory?"

(1 Corinthians 15:51–55, NKJV)

Indeed, we felt within ourselves that we had received the [very] sentence of death, but that was to keep us from trusting in and depending on ourselves instead of on God Who raises the dead.

(2 Corinthians 1:9, Amp)

So we are always confident, knowing that while we are at home in the body we are absent from the Lord. For we walk by faith, not by sight. We are confident, yes, well pleased rather to be absent from the body and to be present with the Lord. Therefore we make it our aim, whether present or absent, to be well pleasing to Him.

(2 Corinthians 5:6–9, nkjv)

For to me, to live is Christ and to die is gain. But if I am to live on in the flesh, this will mean fruitful labor for me; and I do not know which to choose. But I am hard-pressed from both directions, having the desire to depart and be with Christ, for that is very much better.

(Philippians 1:21–23, nasb)

Brothers, we do not want you to be ignorant about those who fall asleep, or to grieve like the rest of men, who have no hope. We believe that Jesus died and rose again and so we believe that God will bring with Jesus those who have fallen asleep in him. For the Lord himself will come down from heaven, with a loud command, with the voice of the archangel and with the trumpet call of God, and the dead in Christ will rise first.

(1 Thessalonians 4:13–14; 16, niv)

Who died for us so that whether we are still alive or are dead [at Christ's appearing], we might live together with Him and share His life.

(1 Thessalonians 5:10, Amp)

For I am already being poured out as a drink offering, and the time of my departure is at hand. I have fought the good fight, I have finished the race, I have kept the faith. Finally, there is laid up for me the crown of righteousness, which the Lord, the righteous Judge, will give to me on that Day, and not to me only but also to all who have loved His appearing.

(2 Timothy 4:6–8, NKJV)

He too shared in their humanity so that by his death he might destroy him who holds the power of death—that is, the devil—and free those who all their lives were held in slavery by their fear of death.

(Hebrews 2:14b–15, NIV)

And just as it is appointed for [all] men once to die, and after that the [certain] judgment, even so it is that Christ, having been offered to take upon Himself and bear as a burden the sins of many once and once for all, will appear a second time, not to carry any burden of sin nor to deal with sin, but to bring to full salvation those who are [eagerly, constantly, and patiently] waiting for and expecting Him.

(Hebrews 9:27–28, Amp)

Then I heard a voice from heaven saying to me, "Write: 'Blessed are the dead who die in the Lord from now on.""Yes," says the Spirit, "that they may rest from their labors, and their works follow them."

(Revelation 14:13, NKJV)

And God will wipe away every tear from their eyes; there shall be no more death, nor sorrow, nor crying. There shall be no more pain, for the former things have passed away.

(Revelation 21:4, NKJV)

Debts
(see Money)

Decisions

Trust in the Lord with all your heart and lean not on your own understanding; in all your ways acknowledge him, and he will make your paths straight.

(Proverbs 3:5–6, NIV)

He who earnestly seeks good finds favor, but trouble will come to him who seeks evil.

(Proverbs 11:27, NKJV)

No one can serve two masters; for either he will hate the one and love the other, or he will be devoted to one and despise the other. You cannot serve God and wealth.

(Matthew 6:24, NASB)

Do not be deceived, God is not mocked; for whatever a

man sows, this he will also reap. For the one who sows to his own flesh will from the flesh reap corruption, but the one who sows to the Spirit will from the Spirit reap eternal life.

(Galatians 6:7–8, NASB)

So any person who knows what is right to do but does not do it, to him it is sin.

(James 4:17, AMP)

Depression
(see also Loneliness and Sorrow)

Oh, that I might have my request, and that God would grant me the thing that I long for! I even wish that it would please God to crush me, that He would let loose His hand and cut me off! Then would I still have consolation—yes, I would leap [for joy] amid unsparing pain [though I shrink from it]—that I have not concealed or denied the words of the Holy One!

(Job 6:8–10, AMP)

The Lord is near to the brokenhearted and saves those who are crushed in spirit.

(Psalm 34:18, NASB)

Why are you downcast, O my soul? Why so disturbed within me? Put your hope in God, for I will yet praise him, my Savior and my God.

(Psalm 43:5, NIV)

Cast your cares on the Lord and he will sustain you; he will never let the righteous fall.

(Psalm 55:22, NIV)

When anxiety was great within me, your consolation brought joy to my soul.

(Psalm 94:19, NIV)

The Lord upholds all who fall, and raises up all who are bowed down.

(Psalm 145:14, NKJV)

He heals the brokenhearted and binds up their wounds.

(Psalm 147:3, NKJV)

A joyful heart makes a cheerful face, but when the heart is sad, the spirit is broken.

(Proverbs 15:13, NASB)

A cheerful heart is good medicine, but a crushed spirit dries up the bones.

(Proverbs 17:22, NIV)

I dwell on a high and holy place, and also with the contrite and lowly of spirit in order to revive the spirit of the lowly and to revive the heart of the contrite.

(Isaiah 57:15b, NASB)

Remember my affliction and roaming, the wormwood and the gall. My soul still remembers and sinks within me. This I recall to my mind, therefore I have hope. Through the Lord's mercies we are not consumed, because His compassions fail not. They are new every morning; great is Your faithfulness. "The Lord is my portion," says my soul, "therefore I hope in Him!"

(Lamentations 3:19–24, NKJV)

And who of you by being worried can add a single hour to his life? So do not worry about tomorrow; for tomorrow will care for itself. Each day has enough trouble of its own.

(Matthew 6:27, 34, NASB)

Do not be anxious about anything, but in everything, by prayer and petition, with thanksgiving, present your requests to God. And the peace of God, which transcends all understanding, will guard your hearts and your minds in Christ Jesus. Finally, brothers, whatever is true, whatever is noble, whatever is right, whatever is pure, whatever is lovely, whatever is admirable—if anything is excellent or praiseworthy—think about such things.

(Philippians 4:6–8, NIV)

For God did not give us a spirit of timidity, but a spirit of power, of love and of self-discipline.

(2 Timothy 1:7, NIV)

Casting all your anxiety on Him, because He cares for you.

(1 Peter 5:7, NASB)

Dieting
(see Weight Control)

Disappointment
(see Discouragement and Comfort in Trouble)

Discipline

His own iniquities shall ensnare the wicked man, and he shall be held with the cords of his sin. He will die for lack of discipline and instruction, and in the greatness of his folly he will go astray and be lost.

(Proverbs 5:22–23, AMP)

Whoever loves instruction loves knowledge, but he who hates correction is stupid.

(Proverbs 12:1, NKJV)

He who refuses and ignores instruction and correction despises himself, but he who heeds reproof gets understanding.

(Proverbs 15:32, AMP)

But when we are judged, we are disciplined by the Lord so that we will not be condemned along with the world.

(1 Corinthians 11:32, NASB)

Moreover, we have all had human fathers who disciplined us and we respected them for it. How much more should we submit to the Father of our spirits and live! Our fathers disciplined us for a little while as they thought best; but God disciplines us for our good, that we may share in his holiness. No discipline seems pleasant at the time, but painful. Later on, however, it produces a harvest of righteousness and peace for those who have been trained by it.

(Hebrews 12:9–11, NIV)

Discouragement
(see also Comfort in Trouble)

Oh, fear the Lord, you His saints! There is no want to those who fear Him. The young lions lack and suffer hunger; but those who seek the Lord shall not lack any good thing.

(Psalm 34:9–10, NKJV)

He will respond to the prayer of the destitute; he will not despise their plea.

(Psalm 102:17, NIV)

For you know the grace of our Lord Jesus Christ, that though He was rich, yet for your sakes He became poor, that you through His poverty might become rich.

(2 Corinthians 8:9, NKJV)

Dishonesty
(see Honesty)

Doubt

And Jesus answered them, Truly I say to you, if you have faith (a firm relying trust) and do not doubt, you will not only do what has been done to the fig tree, but even if you say to this mountain, Be taken up and cast into the sea, it will be done.

(Matthew 21:21, AMP)

I am astonished that you are so quickly deserting the one who called you by the grace of Christ and are turning to a different gospel—which is really no gospel at all. Evidently some people are throwing you into confusion and are trying to pervert the gospel of Christ. But even if we or an angel from heaven should preach a gospel other than the one we preached to you, let him be eternally condemned.

(Galatians 1:6–8, NIV)

See to it, brothers, that none of you has a sinful, unbelieving heart that turns away from the living God.

(Hebrews 3:12, NIV)

But we are not of those who shrink back to destruction, but of those who have faith to the preserving of the soul.

(Hebrews 10:39, NASB)

If any of you lacks wisdom, let him ask of God, who gives to all liberally and without reproach, and it will be given to him. But let him ask in faith, with no doubting, for he who doubts is like a wave of the sea driven and tossed by the wind. For let not that man suppose that he will receive anything from the Lord; he is a double-minded man, unstable in all his ways.

(James 1:5–8, NKJV)

Envy

For anger slays the foolish man, and jealousy kills the simple.

(Job 5:2, NASB)

Fret not yourself because of evildoers, neither be envious against those who work unrighteousness (that which is not upright or in right standing with God). For they shall soon be cut down like the grass, and wither as the green herb.

(Psalm 37:1–2, AMP)

But as for me, my feet came close to stumbling, my steps had almost slipped. For I was envious of the arrogant as I saw the prosperity of the wicked.

(Psalm 73:2–3, NASB)

A calm and undisturbed mind and heart are the life and health of the body, but envy, jealousy, and wrath are like rottenness of the bones.

(Proverbs 14:30, AMP)

Do not let your heart envy sinners, but be zealous for the fear of the Lord all the day.

(Proverbs 23:17, NKJV)

Do not be envious of evil men, nor desire to be with them.

(Proverbs 24:1, NKJV)

Wrath is cruel and anger is an overwhelming flood, but who is able to stand before jealousy?

(Proverbs 27:4, AMP)

Again, I saw that for all toil and every skillful work a man is envied by his neighbor. This also is vanity and grasping for the wind.

(Ecclesiastes 4:4, NKJV)

But if you harbor bitter envy and selfish ambition in your hearts, do not boast about it or deny the truth. Such "wisdom" does not come down from heaven but is earthly, unspiritual, of the devil. For where you have envy and selfish ambition, there you find disorder and every evil practice.

(James 3:14–16, NIV)

Eternal Life
(see also Death and Judgment and Paradise)

For I know that my Redeemer lives, and He shall stand at last on the earth; and after my skin is destroyed, this I know, that in my flesh I shall see God, Whom I shall see for myself, and my eyes shall behold, and not another. How my heart yearns within me!

(Job 19:25–27, NKJV)

For behold, I create new heavens and a new earth. And the former things shall not be remembered or come into mind.

(Isaiah 65:17, AMP)

And Jesus said to them, The people of this world and present age marry and are given in marriage; but those who are considered worthy to gain that other world and that future age and to attain to the resurrection from the dead neither marry nor are given in marriage; for they cannot die again, but they are angel-like and equal to angels. And being sons of and sharers in the resurrection, they are sons of God.

(Luke 20:34–36, AMP)

For God so loved the world that He gave His only begotten Son, that whoever believes in Him should not perish but have everlasting life.

(John 3:16, NKJV)

Do not be surprised and wonder at this, for the time is coming when all those who are in the tombs shall hear His voice, and they shall come out—those who have practiced doing good [will come out] to the resurrection of [new] life, and those who have done evil will be raised for judgment [raised to meet their sentence].

(John 5:28–29, AMP)

Most assuredly, I say to you, he who believes in Me has everlasting life.

(John 6:47, NKJV)

My sheep hear My voice, and I know them, and they follow Me. And I give them eternal life, and they shall never perish; neither shall anyone snatch them out of My hand.

(John 10:27–28, NKJV)

In my Father's house are many mansions; if it were not so, I would have told you. I go to prepare a place for you. And if I go and prepare a place for you, I will come again and receive you to Myself; that where I am, there you may be also.

(John 14:2–3, NKJV)

Just a little while now, and the world will not see Me any more, but you will see Me; because I live, you will live also.

(John 14:19, AMP)

But now that you have been set free from sin and have become slaves to God, the benefit you reap leads to holiness, and the result is eternal life. For the wages of sin is death, but the gift of God is eternal life in Christ Jesus our Lord.

(Romans 6:22–23, NIV)

But if the Spirit of Him who raised Jesus from the dead dwells in you, He who raised Christ from the dead will also give life to your mortal bodies through His Spirit who dwells in you.

(Romans 8:11, NKJV)

Do you not know that in a race all the runners run, but

only one gets the prize? Run in such a way as to get the prize. Everyone who competes in the games goes into strict training. They do it to get a crown that will not last; but we do it to get a crown that will last forever.

(1 Corinthians 9:24–25, NIV)

For we know that if the earthly tent which is our house is torn down, we have a building from God, a house not made with hands, eternal in the heavens.

(2 Corinthians 5:1, NASB)

But our citizenship is in heaven. And we eagerly await a Savior from there, the Lord Jesus Christ, who, by the power that enables him to bring everything under his control, will transform our lowly bodies so that they will be like his glorious body.

(Philippians 3:20–21, NIV)

The saying is sure and worthy of confidence: If we have died with Him, we shall also live with Him. If we endure, we shall also reign with Him. If we deny and disown and reject Him, He will also deny and disown and reject us. If we are faithless [do not believe and are untrue to Him], He remains true (faithful to his Word and His righteous character), for He cannot deny Himself.

(2 Timothy 2:11–13, AMP)

A faith and knowledge resting on the hope of eternal life, which God, who does not lie, promised before the beginning of time.

(Titus 1:2, NIV)

And this is the testimony: that God has given us eternal life, and this life is in His Son. He who has the Son has life; he who does not have the Son of God does not have life. These things I have written to you who believe in the name of the Son of God, that you may know that you have eternal life, and that you may continue to believe in the name of the Son of God.

(1 John 5:11–13, NKJV)

Keep yourselves in God's love as you wait for the mercy of our Lord Jesus Christ to bring you to eternal life.

(Jude 21, NIV)

Therefore they are before the throne of God, and serve Him day and night in His temple. And He who sits on the throne will dwell among them. They shall neither hunger anymore nor thirst anymore; the sun shall not strike them, nor any heat; for the Lamb who is in the midst of the throne will shepherd them and lead them to living fountains of waters. And God will wipe away every tear from their eyes.

(Revelation 7:15–17, NKJV)

Exercise

For bodily exercise profits a little, but godliness is profitable for all things, having promise of the life that now is and of that which is to come.

(1 Timothy 4:8, NKJV)

Faith

So faith comes by hearing [what is told], and what is heard comes by the preaching [of the message that came from the lips] of Christ (the Messiah Himself).

(Romans 10:17, AMP)

And my message and my preaching were not in persuasive words of wisdom, but in demonstration of the Spirit and of power, so that your faith would not rest on the wisdom of men, but on the power of God.

(1 Corinthians 2:4–5, NASB)

We live by faith, not by sight.

(2 Corinthians 5:7, NIV)

For by grace you have been saved through faith; and that not of yourselves, it is the gift of God; not as a result of works, so that no one may boast.

(Ephesians 2:8–9, NASB)

In addition to all this, take up the shield of faith, with which you can extinguish all the flaming arrows of the evil one.

(Ephesians 6:16, NIV)

For we also have had the gospel preached to us, just as they did; but the message they heard was of no value to them because those who heard did not combine it with faith.

(Hebrews 4:2, NIV)

Now faith is being sure of what we hope for and certain of what we do not see.

(Hebrews 11:1, NIV)

And without faith it is impossible to please God, because anyone who comes to him must believe that he exists and that he rewards those who earnestly seek him.

(Hebrews 11:6, NIV)

Let us fix our eyes on Jesus, the author and perfecter of our faith, who for the joy set before him endured the cross, scorning its shame, and sat down at the right hand of the throne of God.

(Hebrews 12:2, NIV)

What use is it, my brethren, if someone says he has faith but he has no works? Can that faith save him? If a brother or sister is without clothing and in need of daily food, and one of you says to them, "Go in peace, be warmed and be filled," and yet you do not give them what is necessary for their body, what use is that? Even so faith, if it has no works, is dead, being by itself.

(James 2:14–17, NASB)

You see then that a man is justified by works, and not by faith only. For as the body without the spirit is dead, so faith without works is dead also.

(James 2:24, 26, NKJV)

For everyone born of God overcomes the world. This is the victory that has overcome the world, even our faith.

(1 John 5:4, NIV)

Faith, Weakness of

For even though by this time you ought to be teaching others, you actually need someone to teach you over again the very first principles of God's Word. You have come to need milk, not solid food. For everyone who continues to feed on milk is obviously inexperienced and unskilled in the doctrine of righteousness (of conformity to the divine will in purpose, thought, and action), for he is a mere infant [not able to talk yet]! But solid food is for full-grown men, for those whose senses and mental faculties are trained by practice to discriminate and distinguish between what is morally good and noble and what is evil and contrary either to divine or human law.

(Hebrews 5:12–14, Amp)

But my righteous one will live by faith. And if he shrinks back, I will not be pleased with him.

(Hebrews 10:38, niv)

For consider Him who endured such hostility from sinners against Himself, lest you become weary and discouraged in your souls.

(Hebrews 12:3, nkjv)

Family
(see also Parenting)

But as for me and my house, we will serve the Lord.

(Joshua 24:15b, nkjv)

Better a dry crust with peace and quiet than a house full of feasting, with strife.

(Proverbs 17:1, NIV)

Through wisdom a house is built, and by understanding it is established.

(Proverbs 24:3, NKJV)

Do not forsake your friend and the friend of your father, and do not go to your brother's house when disaster strikes you—better a neighbor nearby than a brother far away.

(Proverbs 27:10, NIV)

Whoever robs his father or his mother and says, This is no sin—he is in the same class as [an open, lawless robber and] a destroyer.

(Proverbs 28:24, AMP)

Any kingdom divided against itself is laid waste; and a house divided against itself falls.

(Luke 11:17b, NASB)

But if a widow has children or grandchildren, these should learn first of all to put their religion into practice by caring for their own family and so repaying their parents and grandparents, for this is pleasing to God.

(1 Timothy 5:4, NIV)

If anyone fails to provide for his relatives, and especially for those of his own family, he has disowned the faith [by failing to accompany it with fruits] and is worse than an unbeliever [who performs his obligation in these matters].

(1 Timothy 5:8, Amp)

Fear

The Lord is my light and my salvation; whom shall I fear? The Lord is the strength of my life; of whom shall I be afraid?

(Psalm 27:1, nkjv)

I sought the Lord, and He heard me, and delivered me from all my fears.

(Psalm 34:4, nkjv)

In God I have put my trust; I will not be afraid. What can man do to me?

(Psalm 56:11, nkjv)

Fear not, for I am with you; be not dismayed, for I am your God. I will strengthen you, yes, I will help you, I will uphold you with My righteous right hand.

(Isaiah 41:10, nkjv)

And do not fear those who kill the body but cannot kill the soul. But rather fear Him who is able to destroy both soul and body in hell. Are not two sparrows sold for a copper coin? And not one of them falls to the ground apart from your Father's will. But the very hairs of your head are all numbered. Do not fear therefore; you are of more value than many sparrows.

(Matthew 10:28–31, NKJV)

And lo, I am with you always, even to the end of the age.

(Matthew 28:20b, NKJV)

Let not your heart be troubled; you believe in God, believe also in Me.

(John 14:1, NKJV)

For you have not received a spirit of slavery leading to fear again, but you have received a spirit of adoption as sons.

(Romans 8:15a, NASB)

For I am persuaded that neither death nor life, nor angels nor principalities nor powers, nor things present nor things to come, nor height nor depth, nor any other created thing, shall be able to separate us from the love of God which is in Christ Jesus our Lord.

(Romans 8:38–39, NKJV)

For God did not give us a spirit of timidity, but a spirit of power, of love and of self-discipline.

(2 Timothy 1:7, NIV)

There is no fear in love; but perfect love casts out fear, because fear involves punishment, and the one who fears is not perfected in love.

(1 John 4:18, NASB)

Fellowship
(see also Relationships and Loving Others)

I was glad when they said to me, Let us go to the house of the Lord!

(Psalm 122:1, AMP)

For where two or three are gathered together in My name, I am there in the midst of them.

(Matthew 18:20, NKJV)

They were continually devoting themselves to the apostles' teaching and to fellowship, to the breaking of bread and to prayer. Day by day continuing with one mind in the temple, and breaking bread from house to house, they were taking their meals together with gladness and sincerity of heart, praising God and having favor with all the people.

(Acts 2:42; 46–47a, NASB)

Therefore if there is any encouragement in Christ, if there is any consolation of love, if there is any fellowship of the Spirit, if any affection and compassion, make my joy complete by being of the same mind, maintaining the same love, united in spirit, intent on one purpose.

(Philippians 2:1–2, NASB)

But encourage one another day after day, as long as it is still called "Today," so that none of you will be hardened by the deceitfulness of sin.

(Hebrews 3:13, NASB)

And let us consider how we may spur one another on toward love and good deeds. Let us not give up meeting together, as some are in the habit of doing, but let us encourage one another—and all the more as you see the Day approaching.

(Hebrews 10:24–25, NIV)

Finances
(see Money)

Flattery

A lying tongue hates those who are crushed by it, and a flattering mouth works ruin.

(Proverbs 26:28, NKJV)

He who rebukes a man shall afterward find more favor than he who flatters with the tongue.

(Proverbs 28:23, AMP)

A man who flatters his neighbor spreads a net for his feet.

(Proverbs 29:5, NKJV)

Woe to you when all men speak well of you, for their fathers used to treat the false prophets in the same way.

(Luke 6:26, NASB)

For certain persons have crept in unnoticed, those who were long beforehand marked out for this condemnation, ungodly persons who turn the grace of our God into licentiousness and deny our only Master and Lord, Jesus Christ. These are grumblers, finding fault, following after their own lusts; they speak arrogantly, flattering people for the sake of gaining an advantage.

(Jude 4, 16, NASB)

Forgiveness

If My people who are called by My name will humble themselves, and pray and seek My face, and turn from their wicked ways, then I will hear from heaven, and will forgive their sin and heal their land.

(2 Chronicles 7:14, NKJV)

Hide Your face from my sins, and blot out all my iniquities. Create in me a clean heart, O God, and renew a steadfast spirit within me. Do not cast me away from Your presence, and do not take Your Holy Spirit from me. Restore to me the joy of Your salvation, and uphold me by your generous Spirit.

(Psalm 51:9–12, NKJV)

As far as the east is from the west, so far has He removed our transgressions from us.

(Psalm 103:12, AMP)

If you, O Lord, kept a record of sins, O Lord, who could stand? But with you there is forgiveness; therefore you are feared.

(Psalm 130:3–4, NIV)

"Come now, and let us reason together," says the Lord, "though your sins are like scarlet, they shall be as white as snow; though they are red like crimson, they shall be as wool."

(Isaiah 1:18, NKJV)

I, even I, am He who blots out your transgressions for My own sake; and I will not remember your sins.

(Isaiah 43:25, NKJV)

Therefore if you bring your gift to the altar, and there remember that your brother has something against you, leave your gift there before the altar, and go your way. First be reconciled to your brother, and then come and offer your gift.

(Matthew 5:23–24, NKJV)

You have heard that it was said, "You shall love your neighbor and hate your enemy." But I say to you, love your enemies, bless those who curse you, do good to those who hate you, and pray for those who spitefully use you and persecute you, that you may be sons of your Father in heaven; for He makes His sun rise on the evil and on the good, and sends rain on the just and on the unjust.

(Matthew 5:43–45, NKJV)

For if you forgive men their trespasses, your heavenly Father will also forgive you. But if you do not forgive men their trespasses, neither will your Father forgive your trespasses.

(Matthew 6:14–15, NKJV)

Then Peter came to Him and said, "Lord, how often shall my brother sin against me, and I forgive him? Up to seven times?"

Jesus said to him, "I do not say to you up to seven times, but up to seventy times seven."

(Matthew 18:21–22, NKJV)

And whenever you stand praying, if you have anything against anyone, forgive him and let it drop (leave it, let it go), in order that your Father Who is in heaven may also forgive you your [own] failings and shortcomings and let them drop.

(Mark 11:25, AMP)

Take heed to yourselves. If your brother sins against you, rebuke him; and if he repents, forgive him. And if he sins against you seven times in a day, and seven times in a day returns to you, saying, "I repent," you shall forgive him.

(Luke 17:3–4, NKJV)

Therefore let it be known to you, brethren, that through Him forgiveness of sins is proclaimed to you, and through Him everyone who believes is freed from all things, from which you could not be freed through the Law of Moses.

(Acts 13:38–39, NASB)

Blessed and happy and to be envied are those whose iniquities are forgiven and whose sins are covered up and completely buried. Blessed and happy and to be envied is the person of whose sin the Lord will take no account nor reckon it against him.

(Romans 4:7–8, AMP)

Be kind and compassionate to one another, forgiving each other, just as in Christ God forgave you.

(Ephesians 4:32, NIV)

[The Father] has delivered and drawn us to Himself out of the control and the dominion of darkness and has transferred us into the kingdom of the Son of His love, in Whom we have our redemption through His blood, [which means] the forgiveness of our sins.

(Colossians 1:13–14, AMP)

Once you were alienated from God and were enemies in your minds because of your evil behavior. But now he has reconciled you by Christ's physical body through death to present you holy in his sight, without blemish and free from accusation.

(Colossians 1:21–22, NIV)

For I will be merciful and gracious toward their sins and I will remember their deeds of unrighteousness no more.

(Hebrews 8:12, AMP)

If we confess our sins, he is faithful and just and will forgive us our sins and purify us from all unrighteousness.

(1 John 1:9, NIV)

My little children, I am writing these things to you so that you may not sin. And if anyone sins, we have an Advocate with the Father, Jesus Christ the righteous.

(1 John 2:1, NASB)

Forgiveness, Needing

Blessed is he whose transgression is forgiven, whose sin is covered. Blessed is the man to whom the Lord does not impute iniquity, and in whose spirit there is no deceit. When I kept silent, my bones grew old through my groaning all the day long. For day and night Your hand was heavy upon me; my vitality was turned into the drought of summer. I acknowledged my sin to You, and my iniquity I have not hidden. I said, "I will confess my transgressions to the Lord," and You forgave the iniquity of my sin.

(Psalm 32:1–5, NKJV)

All we like sheep have gone astray; we have turned, every one, to his own way; and the Lord has laid on Him the iniquity of us all.

(Isaiah 53:6, NKJV)

Friends, Forsaken by

A despairing man should have the devotion of his friends, even though he forsakes the fear of the Almighty. But my brothers are as undependable as intermittent streams, as the streams that overflow when darkened by thawing ice and swollen with melting snow, but that cease to flow in the dry season, and in the heat vanish from their channels.

(Job 6:14–17, NIV)

I am a dread to my friends—those who see me on the street flee from me. I am forgotten by them as though I were dead. But I trust in you, O Lord; I say, "You are my God." My times are in your hands; deliver me from my enemies and from those who pursue me.

(Psalm 31:11b-12a; 14–15, NIV)

Even my close friend in whom I trusted, who ate my bread, has lifted up his heel against me. But You, O Lord, be gracious to me and raise me up.

(Psalm 41:9–10a, NASB)

You have taken from me my closest friends and have made me repulsive to them. I am confined and cannot escape; my eyes are dim with grief. I call to you, O Lord, every day; I spread out my hands to you. You have taken my companions and loved ones from me; the darkness is my closest friend.

(Psalm 88:8–9; 18, NIV)

Confidence in an unfaithful man in time of trouble is like a broken tooth or a foot out of joint.

(Proverbs 25:19, AMP)

At that moment Jesus said to the crowds, Have you come out with swords and clubs as [you would] against a robber to capture Me? Day after day I was accustomed to sit in the porches and courts of the temple teaching, and you did not arrest Me. But all this has taken place in order that the Scriptures of the prophets might be fulfilled. Then all the disciples deserted Him and, fleeing, escaped.

(Matthew 26:55–56, AMP)

At my first trial no one acted in my defense [as my advocate] or took my part or [even] stood with me, but all forsook me. May it not be charged against them!

(2 Timothy 4:16, AMP)

Friendship
(see also Relationships)

I am a friend to all who fear you, to all who follow your precepts.

(Psalm 119:63, NIV)

The righteous should choose his friends carefully, for the way of the wicked leads them astray.

(Proverbs 12:26, NKJV)

A man who has friends must himself be friendly, but there is a friend who sticks closer than a brother.

(Proverbs 18:24, NKJV)

Oil and perfume rejoice the heart; so does the sweetness of a friend's counsel that comes from the heart.

(Proverbs 27:9, AMP)

Two are better than one because they have a good return for their labor. For if either of them falls, the one will lift up his companion. But woe to the one who falls when there is not another to lift him up.

(Ecclesiastes 4:9–10, NASB)

Generosity
(see also Giving and Hospitality)

He who despises his neighbor sins; but he who has mercy on the poor, happy is he.

(Proverbs 14:21, NKJV)

He who has pity on the poor lends to the Lord, and He will pay back what he has given.

(Proverbs 19:17, NKJV)

He who gives to the poor will not want, but he who hides his eyes [from their want] will have many a curse.

(Proverbs 28:27, AMP)

Then the righteous will answer Him, saying, "Lord, when did we see You hungry and feed You, or thirsty and give

You drink? When did we see You a stranger and take You in, or naked and clothe You? Or when did we see You sick, or in prison, and come to You?"

And the King will answer and say to them, "Assuredly, I say to you, inasmuch as you did it to one of the least of these My brethren, you did it to Me."

(Matthew 25:37–40, NKJV)

Give, and it will be given to you. They will pour into your lap a good measure—pressed down, shaken together, and running over. For by your standard of measure it will be measured to you in return.

(Luke 6:38, NASB)

We want to tell you further, brethren, about the grace (the favor and spiritual blessing) of God which has been evident in the churches of Macedonia [arousing in them the desire to give alms]; for in the midst of an ordeal of severe tribulation, their abundance of joy and their depth of poverty [together] have overflowed in wealth of lavish generosity on their part. For, as I can bear witness, [they gave] according to their ability, yes, and beyond their ability; and [they did it] voluntarily, begging us most insistently for the favor and the fellowship of contributing in this ministration for [the relief and support of] the saints [in Jerusalem]. Nor [was this gift of theirs merely the contribution] that we expected, but first they gave themselves to the Lord and to us [as His agents] by the will of God [entirely disregarding their personal interests, they gave as much as they possibly could, having put themselves at our disposal to be directed by the will of God].

(2 Corinthians 8:1–5, Amp)

Each man should give what he has decided in his heart to give, not reluctantly or under compulsion, for God loves a cheerful giver.

(2 Corinthians 9:7, niv)

This service that you perform is not only supplying the needs of God's people but is also overflowing in many expressions of thanks to God. Because of the service by which you have proved yourselves, men will praise God for the obedience that accompanies your confession of the gospel of Christ, and for your generosity in sharing with them and with everyone else.

(2 Corinthians 9:12–13, niv)

As for the rich in this world, charge them not to be proud and arrogant and contemptuous of others, nor to set their hopes on uncertain riches, but on God, Who richly and ceaselessly provides us with everything for [our] enjoyment. [Charge them] to do good, to be rich in good works, to be liberal and generous of heart, ready to share [with others].

(1 Timothy 6:17–18, Amp)

But do not forget to do good and to share, for with such sacrifices God is well pleased.

(Hebrews 13:16, NKJV)

Generosity, Hidden Agenda

Many will seek the favor of a generous man, and every man is a friend to him who gives gifts.

(Proverbs 19:6, NASB)

Take heed that you do not do your charitable deeds before men, to be seen by them. Otherwise you have no reward from your Father in heaven. Therefore, when you do a charitable deed, do not sound a trumpet before you as the hypocrites do in the synagogues and in the streets, that they may have glory from men. Assuredly, I say to you, they have their reward. But when you do a charitable deed, do not let your left hand know what your right hand is doing, that your charitable deed may be in secret; and your Father who sees in secret will Himself reward you openly.

(Matthew 6:1–4, NKJV)

Giving
(see also Generosity and Hospitality)

One man gives freely, yet gains even more; another withholds unduly, but comes to poverty. A generous man will prosper; he who refreshes others will himself be refreshed.

(Proverbs 11:24–25, NIV)

And He sat down opposite the treasury, and began observing how the people were putting money into the treasury; and many rich people were putting in large sums. A poor widow came and put in two small copper coins, which amount to a cent. Calling His disciples to Him, He said to them, "Truly I say to you, this poor widow put in more than all the contributors to the treasury; for they all put in out of their surplus, but she, out of her poverty, put in all she owned, all she had to live on."

(Mark 12:41–44, NASB)

From everyone who has been given much, much will be demanded; and from the one who has been entrusted with much, much more will be asked.

(Luke 12:48b, NIV)

It is more blessed to give than to receive.

(Acts 20:35b, NKJV)

Who has ever given to God, that God should repay him? For from him and through him and to him are all things. To him be the glory forever!Amen.

(Romans 11:35–36, NIV)

For if the [eager] readiness to give is there, then it is acceptable and welcomed in proportion to what a person has, not according to what he does not have.

(2 Corinthians 8:12, AMP)

Remember this: Whoever sows sparingly will also reap sparingly, and whoever sows generously will also reap generously. Each man should give what he has decided in his heart to give, not reluctantly or under compulsion, for God loves a cheerful giver.

(2 Corinthians 9:6–7, NIV)

God, Finding

The Lord is with you while you are with Him. If you seek Him, He will be found by you; but if you forsake Him, He will forsake you.

(2 Chronicles 15:2b, NKJV)

And those who know Your name will put their trust in You; for You, Lord, have not forsaken those who seek You.

(Psalm 9:10, NKJV)

How blessed are those who observe His testimonies, who seek Him with all their heart.

(Psalm 119:2, NASB)

You know my sitting down and my rising up; You understand my thought afar off. You comprehend my path and my lying down, and are acquainted with all my ways. For there is not a word on my tongue, but behold, O Lord, You know it altogether. Where can I go from Your Spirit? Or where can I flee from Your presence?

(Psalm 139:2–4; 7, NKJV)

The Lord is near to all who call upon Him, to all who call upon Him in truth.

(Psalm 145:18, NKJV)

I love those who love me, and those who seek me diligently will find me.

(Proverbs 8:17, NKJV)

For whoever finds me finds life and receives favor from the Lord. But whoever fails to find me harms himself; all who hate me love death.

(Proverbs 8:35–36, NIV)

Seek the Lord while He may be found, call upon Him while He is near.

(Isaiah 55:6, NKJV)

Then you will call, and the Lord will answer; you will cry for help, and he will say: Here am I.

(Isaiah 58:9a, NIV)

And you will seek Me and find Me, when you search for Me with all your heart.

(Jeremiah 29:13, NKJV)

The Lord is good to those who wait for Him, to the person who seeks Him.

(Lamentations 3:25, NASB)

Jesus said to him, "I am the way, the truth, and the life. No one comes to the Father except through Me."

(John 14:6, NKJV)

God did this so that men would seek him and perhaps reach out for him and find him, though he is not far from each one of us. For in him we live and move and have our being. As some of your own poets have said, "We are his offspring."

(Acts 17:27–28, NIV)

And without faith it is impossible to please God, because anyone who comes to him must believe that he exists and that he rewards those who earnestly seek him.

(Hebrews 11:6, NIV)

You adulterous people, don't you know that friendship with the world is hatred toward God? Anyone who chooses to be a friend of the world becomes an enemy of God. Come near to God and he will come near to you.

(James 4:4; 8a, NIV)

Behold, I stand at the door and knock. If anyone hears My voice and opens the door, I will come in to him and dine with him, and he with Me.

(Revelation 3:20, NKJV)

Gossip
(see also Speech, Careless)

You shall not go up and down as a dispenser of gossip and scandal among your people.

(Leviticus 19:16a, AMP)

Whoever of you loves life and desires to see many good days, keep your tongue from evil and your lips from speaking lies.

(Psalm 34:12–13, NIV)

A gossip betrays a confidence, but a trustworthy man keeps a secret.

(Proverbs 11:13, NIV)

A perverse man stirs up dissension, and a gossip separates close friends.

(Proverbs 16:28, NIV)

The words of a whisperer are like dainty morsels, and they go down into the innermost parts of the body.

(Proverbs 18:8, NASB)

A gossip betrays a confidence; so avoid a man who talks too much.

(Proverbs 20:19, NIV)

He who guards his mouth and his tongue keeps himself from troubles.

(Proverbs 21:23, AMP)

Without wood a fire goes out; without gossip a quarrel dies down.

(Proverbs 26:20, NIV)

If anyone thinks himself to be religious, and yet does not bridle his tongue but deceives his own heart, this man's religion is worthless.

(James 1:26, NASB)

So also the tongue is a small part of the body, and yet it boasts of great things. See how great a forest is set aflame by such a small fire! And the tongue is a fire, the very world of iniquity; the tongue is set among our members as that which defiles the entire body, and sets on fire the course of our life, and is set on fire by hell. For every species of beasts and birds, of reptiles and creatures of the sea, is tamed and has been tamed by the human race. But no one can tame the tongue; it is a restless evil and full of deadly poison. With it we bless our Lord and Father, and with it we curse men, who have been made in the likeness of God; from the same mouth come both blessing and cursing. My brethren, these things ought not to be this way.

(James 3:5–10, NASB)

Government
(see Church and State)

Greed
(see also Money)

Whoever loves money never has money enough; whoever loves wealth is never satisfied with his income. This too is meaningless.

(Ecclesiastes 5:10, NIV)

What good will it be for a man if he gains the whole world, yet forfeits his soul? Or what can a man give in exchange for his soul?

(Matthew 16:26, NIV)

Then He said to them, "Beware, and be on your guard against every form of greed; for not even when one has an abundance does his life consist of his possessions."

(Luke 12:15, NASB)

Nobody should seek his own good, but the good of others.

(1 Corinthians 10:24, NIV)

For of this you can be sure: No immoral, impure or greedy person—such a man is an idolater—has any inheritance in the kingdom of Christ and of God.

(Ephesians 5:5, NIV)

Grief
(see Sorrow)

Grudges
(see Forgiveness and Revenge)

Guidance

For this is God, our God forever and ever; He will be our guide even to death.

(Psalm 48:14, NKJV)

Direct my footsteps according to your word; let no sin rule over me.

(Psalm 119:133, NIV)

Search me [thoroughly], O God, and know my heart! Try me and know my thoughts! And see if there is any wicked or hurtful way in me, and lead me in the way everlasting.

(Psalm 139:23–24, AMP)

Let me hear Your lovingkindness in the morning; for I trust in You; teach me the way in which I should walk; for to You I lift up my soul.

(Psalm 143:8, NASB)

The mind of man plans his way, but the Lord directs his steps.

(Proverbs 16:9, NASB)

Whether you turn to the right or to the left, your ears will hear a voice behind you, saying, "This is the way; walk in it."

(Isaiah 30:21, NIV)

I am the Lord your God, who teaches you what is best for you, who directs you in the way you should go.

(Isaiah 48:17b, NIV)

I know, O Lord, that a man's life is not his own; it is not for man to direct his steps.

(Jeremiah 10:23, NIV)

Let us fix our eyes on Jesus, the author and perfecter of our faith.

(Hebrews 12:2a, NIV)

Happiness

You turned my wailing into dancing; you removed my sackcloth and clothed me with joy. O Lord my God, I will give you thanks forever.

(Psalm 30:11, 12b, NIV)

Those who look to him are radiant; their faces are never covered with shame.

(Psalm 34:5, NIV)

Delight yourself also in the Lord, and He shall give you the desires of your heart.

(Psalm 37:4, NKJV)

You love righteousness and hate wickedness; therefore God, Your God, has anointed You with the oil of gladness more than Your companions.

(Psalm 45:7, NKJV)

But let the righteous be glad; let them exult before God; yes, let them rejoice with gladness.

(Psalm 68:3, NASB)

Light is sown like seed for the righteous and gladness for the upright in heart.

(Psalm 97:11, NASB)

A cheerful heart is good medicine, but a crushed spirit dries up the bones.

(Proverbs 17:22, NIV)

Without having seen Him, you love Him; though you do not [even] now see Him, you believe in Him and exult and thrill with inexpressible and glorious (triumphant, heavenly) joy. [At the same time] you receive the result (outcome, consummation) of your faith, the salvation of your souls.

(1 Peter 1:8–9, AMP)

Hardship
(see also Trouble)

For affliction does not come from the dust, nor does trouble spring from the ground; yet man is born to trouble, as the sparks fly upward. But as for me, I would seek God, and to God I would commit my cause.

(Job 5:6–8, NKJV)

Your faithfulness continues through all generations; you established the earth, and it endures. Your laws endure to this day, for all things serve you. If your law had not been my delight, I would have perished in my affliction.

(Psalm 119:90–92, NIV)

Though the fig tree does not bud and there are no grapes on the vines, though the olive crop fails and the fields produce no food, though there are no sheep in the pen and no cattle in the stalls, yet I will rejoice in the Lord, I will be joyful in God my Savior.

(Habakkuk 3:17–18, NIV)

These things I have spoken to you, that in Me you may have peace. In the world you will have tribulation; but be of good cheer, I have overcome the world.

(John 16:33, NKJV)

Rejoice and exult in hope; be steadfast and patient in suffering and tribulation; be constant in prayer.

(Romans 12:12, AMP)

Endure hardship as discipline; God is treating you as sons. For what son is not disciplined by his father? Moreover, we have all had human fathers who disciplined us and we respected them for it. How much more should we submit to the Father of our spirits and live!

(Hebrews 12:7, 9, NIV)

Consider it pure joy, my brothers, whenever you face trials of many kinds, because you know that the testing of your faith develops perseverance. Perseverance must finish its work so that you may be mature and complete, not lacking anything. Blessed is the man who perseveres under trial, because when he has stood the test, he will receive the crown of life that God has promised to those who love him.

(James 1:2–4; 12, NIV)

For it is better, if it is the will of God, to suffer for doing good than for doing evil.

(1 Peter 3:17, NKJV)

Hate

Better is a dish of vegetables where love is than a fattened ox served with hatred.

(Proverbs 15:17, NASB)

You have heard that it was said, "Love your neighbor and hate your enemy." But I tell you: Love your enemies and pray for those who persecute you, that you may be sons of your Father in heaven.

(Matthew 5:43–45a, NIV)

But he who hates his brother is in darkness and walks in darkness, and does not know where he is going, because the darkness has blinded his eyes.

(1 John 2:11, NKJV)

By this the children of God and the children of the devil are obvious: anyone who does not practice righteousness is not of God, nor the one who does not love his brother. Everyone who hates his brother is a murderer; and you know that no murderer has eternal life abiding in him.

(1 John 3: 10, 15, NASB)

If someone says, "I love God," and hates his brother, he is a liar; for he who does not love his brother whom he has seen, how can he love God whom he has not seen?

And this commandment we have from Him: that he who loves God must love his brother also.

(1 John 4:20–21, NKJV)

Heaven
(see Eternal Life and Judgment and Paradise)

Health
(see Sickness)

Hell
(see Judgment)

Honesty

Do not steal. Do not lie. Do not deceive one another.

(Leviticus 19:11, NIV)

Such is the end of all who go after ill-gotten gain; it takes away the lives of those who get it.

(Proverbs 1:19, NIV)

He who walks uprightly walks securely, but he who takes a crooked way shall be found out and punished.

(Proverbs 10:9, AMP)

Better is a little with righteousness than great income with injustice.

(Proverbs 16:8, NASB)

He who walks righteously and speaks what is right, who rejects gain from extortion and keeps his hand from accepting bribes, who stops his ears against plots of murder and shuts his eyes against contemplating evil—this is the man who will dwell on the heights, whose refuge will be the mountain fortress. His bread will be supplied, and water will not fail him.

(Isaiah 33:15–16, NIV)

Whoever can be trusted with very little can also be trusted with much, and whoever is dishonest with very little will also be dishonest with much.

(Luke 16:10, NIV)

Well then, you who teach others, do you not teach yourself? While you teach against stealing, do you steal (take what does not really belong to you)?

(Romans 2:21, AMP)

Finally, brothers, whatever is true, whatever is noble, whatever is right, whatever is pure, whatever is lovely, whatever is admirable—if anything is excellent or praiseworthy—think about such things.

(Philippians 4:8, NIV)

Hope

I rise before the dawning of the morning, and cry for help; I hope in Your word.

(Psalm 119:147, NKJV)

The Lord takes pleasure in those who reverently and worshipfully fear Him, in those who hope in His mercy and loving-kindness.

(Psalm 147:11, Amp)

Hope deferred makes the heart sick, but when the desire is fulfilled, it is a tree of life.

(Proverbs 13:12, Amp)

For in hope we have been saved, but hope that is seen is not hope; for who hopes for what he already sees? But if we hope for what we do not see, with perseverance we wait eagerly for it.

(Romans 8:24–25, NASB)

For everything that was written in the past was written to teach us, so that through endurance and the encouragement of the Scriptures we might have hope.

(Romans 15:4, NIV)

We are hard-pressed on every side, yet not crushed; we are perplexed, but not in despair; persecuted, but not forsaken; struck down, but not destroyed.

(2 Corinthians 4:8–9, NKJV)

Recalling unceasingly before our God and Father your work energized by faith and service motivated by love and unwavering hope in [the return of] our Lord Jesus Christ (the Messiah).

(1 Thessalonians 1:3, Amp)

But Christ was faithful as a Son over His house—whose house we are, if we hold fast our confidence and the boast of our hope firm until the end.

(Hebrews 3:6, NASB)

Because God wanted to make the unchanging nature of his purpose very clear to the heirs of what was promised, he confirmed it with an oath. God did this so that, by two unchangeable things in which it is impossible for God to lie, we who have fled to take hold of the hope offered to us may be greatly encouraged. We have this hope as an anchor for the soul, firm and secure.

(Hebrews 6:17–19a, NIV)

Therefore, prepare your minds for action, keep sober in spirit, fix your hope completely on the grace to be brought to you at the revelation of Jesus Christ.

(1 Peter 1:13, NASB)

Hospitality
(see also Generosity and Giving)

Contribute to the needs of God's people [sharing in the necessities of the saints]; pursue the practice of hospitality.

(Romans 12:13, AMP)

Do not neglect to show hospitality to strangers, for by this some have entertained angels without knowing it.

(Hebrews 13:2, NASB)

Offer hospitality to one another without grumbling. Each one should use whatever gift he has received to serve others, faithfully administering God's grace in its various forms.

(1 Peter 4:9–10, NIV)

Beloved, you are acting faithfully in whatever you accomplish for the brethren, and especially when they are strangers; and they have testified to your love before the church. You will do well to send them on their way in a manner worthy of God. For they went out for the sake of the Name, accepting nothing from the Gentiles. Therefore we ought to support such men, so that we may be fellow workers with the truth.

(3 John 5–8, NASB)

Humility

Though the Lord is on high, yet He regards the lowly; but the proud He knows from afar.

(Psalm 138:6, NKJV)

When pride comes, then comes disgrace, but with humility comes wisdom.

(Proverbs 11:2, NIV)

The reverent and worshipful fear of the Lord brings instruction in Wisdom, and humility comes before honor.

(Proverbs 15:33, AMP)

Better it is to be of a humble spirit with the meek and poor than to divide the spoil with the proud.

(Proverbs 16:19, AMP)

The reward of humility and the reverent and worshipful fear of the Lord is riches and honor and life.

(Proverbs 22:4, AMP)

A man's pride will bring him low, but the humble in spirit will retain honor.

(Proverbs 29:23, NKJV)

He has shown you, O man, what is good; and what does the Lord require of you but to do justly, to love mercy, and to walk humbly with your God?

(Micah 6:8, NKJV)

Blessed are the meek, for they shall inherit the earth.

(Matthew 5:5, NKJV)

Therefore whoever humbles himself as this little child is the greatest in the kingdom of heaven.

(Matthew 18:4, NKJV)

And whoever exalts himself will be humbled, and he who humbles himself will be exalted.

(Matthew 23:12, NKJV)

Let this mind be in you which was also in Christ Jesus, who, being in the form of God, did not consider it robbery to be equal with God, but made Himself of no reputation, taking the form of a bondservant, and coming in the likeness of men. And being found in appearance as a man, He humbled Himself and became obedient to the point of death, even the death of the cross.

(Philippians 2:5–8, NKJV)

Humble yourselves in the sight of the Lord, and He will lift you up.

(James 4:10, NKJV)

Therefore humble yourselves under the mighty hand of God, that He may exalt you at the proper time.

(1 Peter 5:6, NASB)

Husband and Wife

A virtuous and worthy wife [earnest and strong in character] is a crowning joy to her husband, but she who makes him ashamed is as rottenness in his bones.

(Proverbs 12:4, AMP)

House and riches are the inheritance from fathers, but a wise, understanding, and prudent wife is from the Lord.

(Proverbs 19:14, AMP)

Better to live in a desert than with a quarrelsome and ill-tempered wife.

(Proverbs 21:19, NIV)

Who can find a virtuous wife? For her worth is far above rubies. The heart of her husband safely trusts her; so he will have no lack of gain. She does him good and not evil all the days of her life. She opens her mouth with wisdom, and on her tongue is the law of kindness. She watches over the ways of her household, and does not eat the bread of idleness. Her children rise up and call her blessed; her husband also, and he praises her.

(Proverbs 31:10–12; 26–28, NKJV)

And He answered and said to them, "Have you not read that He who made them at the beginning 'made them male and female,' and said, 'For this reason a man shall leave his father and mother and be joined to his wife, and the two shall become one flesh'? "So then, they are no longer two but one flesh. Therefore what God has joined together, let not man separate."

(Matthew 19:4–6, NKJV)

Let the husband render to his wife the affection due her, and likewise also the wife to her husband.

(1 Corinthians 7:3, NKJV)

Wives, submit to your own husbands, as to the Lord. For the husband is head of the wife, as also Christ is head of the church; and He is the Savior of the body. Therefore, just as the church is subject to Christ, so let the wives be to their own husbands in everything. Husbands, love your wives, just as Christ also loved the church and gave Himself for her, that He might sanctify and cleanse her with the washing of water by the word, that He might present her to Himself a glorious church, not having spot or wrinkle or any such thing, but that she should be holy and without blemish. So husbands ought to love their own wives as their own bodies; he who loves his wife loves himself. For no one ever hated his own flesh, but nourishes and cherishes it, just as the Lord does the church. For we are members of His body, of His flesh and of His bones. "For this reason a man shall leave his father and mother and be joined to his wife, and the two shall become one flesh." Nevertheless let each one of you in particular so love his own wife as himself, and let the wife see that she respects her husband.

(Ephesians 5:22–31; 33, NKJV)

Wives, submit to your own husbands, as is fitting in the Lord. Husbands, love your wives and do not be bitter toward them.

(Colossians 3:18–19, NKJV)

In the same way, you wives, be submissive to your own husbands so that even if any of them are disobedient to the word, they may be won without a word by the behavior of their wives, as they observe your chaste and respectful behavior. You husbands in the same way, live with your wives in an understanding way, as with someone weaker, since she is a woman; and show her honor as a fellow heir of the grace of life, so that your prayers will not be hindered.

(1 Peter 3:1–2; 7, NASB)

Hypocrisy
(see also Judging Others)

The Lord says: "These people come near to me with their mouth and honor me with their lips, but their hearts are far from me. Their worship of me is made up only of rules taught by men."

(Isaiah 29:13, NIV)

Why does the way of the wicked prosper? Why are all they at ease and thriving who deal very treacherously and deceitfully? You have planted them, yes, they have taken root; they grow, yes, they bring forth fruit. You are near in their mouths but far from their hearts.

(Jeremiah 12:1c-2, AMP)

And why do you look at the speck in your brother's eye, but do not consider the plank in your own eye? Or how can you say to your brother, "Let me remove the speck from your eye"; and look, a plank is in your own eye? Hypocrite! First remove the plank from your own eye, and then you will see clearly to remove the speck from your brother's eye.

(Matthew 7:3–5, NKJV)

These people draw near Me with their mouths and honor Me with their lips, but their hearts hold off and are far away from Me. Uselessly do they worship Me, for they teach as doctrines the commands of men.

(Matthew 15:8–9, AMP)

Then Jesus said to the crowds and to his disciples: "The teachers of the law and the Pharisees sit in Moses' seat. So you must obey them and do everything they tell you. But do not do what they do, for they do not practice what they preach."

(Matthew 23:1–3, NIV)

So you, too, outwardly appear righteous to men, but inwardly you are full of hypocrisy and lawlessness.

(Matthew 23:28, NASB)

And He said to them, "You are those who justify yourselves before men, but God knows your hearts."

(Luke 16:15a, NKJV)

They profess to know God, but by their deeds they deny Him, being detestable and disobedient and worthless for any good deed.

(Titus 1:16, NASB)

So be done with every trace of wickedness (depravity, malignity) and all deceit and insincerity (pretense, hypocrisy) and grudges (envy, jealousy) and slander and evil speaking of every kind.

(1 Peter 2:1, AMP)

Insecurity
(see Doubt and Depression)

Insomnia

I lie down and sleep; I wake again, because the Lord sustains me.

(Psalm 3:5, NIV)

In peace I will both lie down and sleep, for You alone, O Lord, make me to dwell in safety.

(Psalm 4:8, NASB)

My son, let them not escape from your sight, but keep sound and godly Wisdom and discretion, and they will be life to your inner self, and a gracious ornament to your neck (your outer self). Then you will walk in your way securely and in confident trust, and you shall not dash your foot or stumble. When you lie down, you shall not be afraid; yes, you shall lie down, and your sleep shall be sweet.

(Proverbs 3:21–24, AMP)

For what does a man get in all his labor and in his striving with which he labors under the sun? Because all his days his task is painful and grievous; even at night his mind does not rest. This too is vanity. There is nothing better for a man than to eat and drink and tell himself that his labor is good. This also I have seen that it is from the hand of God. For who can eat and who can have enjoyment without Him?

(Ecclesiastes 2:22–25, NASB)

The sleep of a laboring man is sweet, whether he eats little or much; but the abundance of the rich will not permit him to sleep.

(Ecclesiastes 5:12, NKJV)

Jealousy
(see Envy)

Joy
(see Happiness)

Judging Others
(see also Hypocrisy)

Then David's anger burned greatly against the man, and he said to Nathan, "As the Lord lives, surely the man who has done this deserves to die. He must make restitution for the lamb fourfold, because he did this thing and had no compassion."

Nathan then said to David, "You are the man!"

(2 Samuel 12:5–7a, NASB)

Do not judge and criticize and condemn others, so that you may not be judged and criticized and condemned yourselves. For just as you judge and criticize and condemn others, you will be judged and criticized and condemned, and in accordance with the measure you [use to] deal out to others, it will be dealt out again to you.

(Matthew 7:1–2, AMP)

Do not judge according to appearance, but judge with righteous judgment.

(John 7:24, NASB)

Therefore you have no excuse, everyone of you who passes judgment, for in that which you judge another, you condemn yourself; for you who judge practice the same things.

(Romans 2:1, NASB)

Now accept the one who is weak in faith, but not for the purpose of passing judgment on his opinions.

(Romans 14:1, NASB)

Do not speak evil of one another, brethren. He who speaks evil of a brother and judges his brother, speaks evil of the law and judges the law. But if you judge the law, you are not a doer of the law but a judge. There is one Lawgiver, who is able to save and to destroy. Who are you to judge another?

(James 4:11–12, NKJV)

Judgment
(see also Death and Eternal Life and Paradise)

For God will bring every act to judgment, everything which is hidden, whether it is good or evil.

(Ecclesiastes 12:14, NASB)

So it will be at the end of the age; the angels will come forth and take out the wicked from among the righteous, and will throw them into the furnace of fire; in that place there will be weeping and gnashing of teeth.

(Matthew 13:49–50, NASB)

But of that day and hour no one knows, not even the angels of heaven, but My Father only. Then two men will be in the field: one will be taken and the other left. Two women will be grinding at the mill: one will be taken and the other left. Watch therefore, for you do not know what hour your Lord is coming.

(Matthew 24:36; 40–42, NKJV)

When the Son of Man comes in His glory, and all the holy angels with Him, then He will sit on the throne of His glory. All the nations will be gathered before Him, and He will separate them one from another, as a shepherd divides his sheep from the goats. And He will set the sheep on His right hand, but the goats on the left. Then the King will say to those on His right hand, "Come, you blessed of My Father, inherit the kingdom prepared for you from the foundation of the world." Then He will also say to those on the left hand, "Depart from Me, you cursed, into the everlasting fire prepared for the devil and his angels." And these will go away into everlasting punishment, but the righteous into eternal life."

(Matthew 25:31–34; 41, 46, NKJV)

"There will be signs in sun and moon and stars, and on the earth dismay among nations, in perplexity at the roaring of the sea and the waves, men fainting from fear and the expectation of the things which are coming upon the world; for the powers of the heavens will be shaken. Then they will see the Son of Man coming in a cloud with power and great glory. But when these things begin to take place, straighten up and lift up your heads, because your redemption is drawing near." Then He told them a parable: "Behold the fig tree and all the trees; as soon as they put forth leaves, you see it and know for yourselves that summer is now near. So you also, when you see these things happening, recognize that the kingdom of God is near."

(Luke 21:25–31, NASB)

If anyone hears My teachings and fails to observe them [does not keep them, but disregards them], it is not I who judges him. For I have not come to judge and to condemn and to pass sentence and to inflict penalty on the world, but to save the world. Anyone who rejects Me and persistently sets Me at naught, refusing to accept My teachings, has his judge [however]; for the [very] message that I have spoken will itself judge and convict him at the last day.

(John 12:47–48, AMP)

Because He has fixed a day in which He will judge the world in righteousness through a Man whom He has appointed, having furnished proof to all men by raising Him from the dead.

(Acts 17:31, NASB)

But because of your stubbornness and unrepentant heart you are storing up wrath for yourself in the day of wrath and revelation of the righteous judgment of God, who will render to each person according to his deeds: to those who by perseverance in doing good seek for glory and honor and immortality, eternal life; but to those who are selfishly ambitious and do not obey the truth, but obey unrighteousness, wrath and indignation.

(Romans 2:5–8, NASB)

You, then, why do you judge your brother? Or why do you look down on your brother? For we will all stand before God's judgment seat. It is written: "As surely as I live," says the Lord, "every knee will bow before me; every tongue will confess to God." So then, each of us will give an account of himself to God. Therefore let us stop passing judgment on one another. Instead, make up your mind not to put any stumbling block or obstacle in your brother's way.

(Romans 14:10–13, NIV)

For we must all appear and be revealed as we are before the judgment seat of Christ, so that each one may receive [his pay] according to what he has done in the body, whether good or evil [considering what his purpose and motive have been, and what he has achieved, been busy with, and given himself and his attention to accomplishing].

(2 Corinthians 5:10, AMP)

Nothing in all creation is hidden from God's sight. Everything is uncovered and laid bare before the eyes of him to whom we must give account.

(Hebrews 4:13, NIV)

Speak and act as those who are going to be judged by the law that gives freedom, because judgment without

mercy will be shown to anyone who has not been merciful. Mercy triumphs over judgment.

(James 2:12–13, NIV)

And when the Chief Shepherd appears, you will receive
the crown of glory that does not fade away.

(1 Peter 5:4, NKJV)

But by His word the present heavens and earth are
being reserved for fire, kept for the day of judgment and
destruction of ungodly men.

(2 Peter 3:7, NASB)

But the day of the Lord will come as a thief in the night,
in which the heavens will pass away with a great noise,
and the elements will melt with fervent heat; but the earth
and the works that are in it will be burned up. Therefore,
since all these things will be dissolved, what manner of
persons ought you to be in holy conduct and godliness,
looking for and hastening the coming of the day of God,
because of which the heavens will be dissolved, being on
fire, and the elements will melt with fervent heat? Nevertheless we, according to His promise, look for new heavens and a new earth in which righteousness dwells.

(2 Peter 3:10–13, NKJV)

And I saw the dead, small and great, standing before God,
and books were opened. And another book was opened,
which is the Book of Life. And the dead were judged
according to their works, by the things which were written in the books. The sea gave up the dead who were in
it, and Death and Hades delivered up the dead who were

in them. And they were judged, each one according to his works. Then Death and Hades were cast into the lake of fire. This is the second death. And anyone not found written in the Book of Life was cast into the lake of fire.

(Revelation 20:12–15, NKJV)

Nothing impure will ever enter it, nor will anyone who does what is shameful or deceitful, but only those whose names are written in the Lamb's book of life.

(Revelation 21:27, NIV)

Behold, I am coming soon, and I shall bring My wages and rewards with Me, to repay and render to each one just what his own actions and his own work merit.

(Revelation 22:12, AMP)

Kindness
(see Character)

Knowledge
(see Wisdom)

Laziness

Go to the ant, you sluggard! Consider her ways and be wise.

(Proverbs 6:6, NKJV)

Lazy hands make a man poor, but diligent hands bring wealth.

(Proverbs 10:4, NIV)

The soul of a lazy man desires, and has nothing; but the soul of the diligent shall be made rich.

(Proverbs 13:4, NKJV)

The way of the lazy is as a hedge of thorns, but the path of the upright is a highway.

(Proverbs 15:19, NASB)

The lazy man will not plow because of winter; he will beg during harvest and have nothing.

(Proverbs 20:4, NKJV)

Do not love sleep or you will grow poor; stay awake and you will have food to spare.

(Proverbs 20:13, NIV)

The desire of the lazy man kills him, for his hands refuse to labor.

(Proverbs 21:25, NKJV)

A little sleep, a little slumber, a little folding of the hands to rest; so shall your poverty come like a prowler, and your need like an armed man.

(Proverbs 24:33–34, NKJV)

He who cultivates his land will have plenty of bread, but

he who follows worthless people and pursuits will have poverty enough.

(Proverbs 28:19, AMP)

The fool folds his hands together and eats his own flesh [destroying himself by indolence].

(Ecclesiastes 4:5, AMP)

He who observes the wind [and waits for all conditions to be favorable] will not sow, and he who regards the clouds will not reap.

(Ecclesiastes 11:4, AMP)

Never lag in zeal and in earnest endeavor; be aglow and burning with the Spirit, serving the Lord.

(Romans 12:11, AMP)

Let the thief steal no more, but rather let him be industrious, making an honest living with his own hands, so that he may be able to give to those in need.

(Ephesians 4:28, AMP)

For even when we were with you, we used to give you this order: if anyone is not willing to work, then he is not to eat, either. For we hear that some among you are leading an undisciplined life, doing no work at all, but acting like busybodies. Now such persons we command and exhort in the Lord Jesus Christ to work in quiet fashion and eat their own bread.

(2 Thessalonians 3:10–12, NASB)

Loneliness
(see also Depression and Sorrow)

[Lord] turn to me and be gracious to me, for I am lonely and afflicted.

(Psalm 25:16, Amp)

There was a certain man without a dependent, having neither a son nor a brother, yet there was no end to all his labor. Indeed, his eyes were not satisfied with riches and he never asked, "And for whom am I laboring and depriving myself of pleasure?" This too is vanity and it is a grievous task.

(Ecclesiastes 4:8, nasb)

For none of us lives to himself alone and none of us dies to himself alone.

(Romans 14:7, niv)

Loving God

He who has My commandments and keeps them is the one who loves Me; and he who loves Me will be loved by My Father, and I will love him and will disclose Myself to him.

(John 14:21, nasb)

And we know that in all things God works for the good of those who love him, who have been called according to his purpose.

(Romans 8:28, niv)

Do not love the world or the things in the world. If anyone loves the world, the love of the Father is not in him.

(1 John 2:15, NKJV)

In this is love: not that we loved God, but that He loved us and sent His Son to be the propitiation (the atoning sacrifice) for our sins.

(1 John 4:10, AMP)

We love Him because He first loved us.

(1 John 4:19, NKJV)

For this is the love of God, that we keep His commandments; and His commandments are not burdensome.

(1 John 5:3, NASB)

Loving Others
(see also Relationships)

My command is this: Love each other as I have loved you. Greater love has no one than this, that he lay down his life for his friends.

(John 15:12–13, NIV)

Be devoted to one another in brotherly love. Honor one another above yourselves.

(Romans 12:10, NIV)

Love does no harm to a neighbor; therefore love is the fulfillment of the law.

(Romans 13:10, NKJV)

Love is patient, love is kind. It does not envy, it does not boast, it is not proud. It is not rude, it is not self-seeking, it is not easily angered, it keeps no record of wrongs. Love does not delight in evil but rejoices with the truth. It always protects, always trusts, always hopes, always perseveres.

(1 Corinthians 13:4–7, NIV)

The entire law is summed up in a single command: "Love your neighbor as yourself."

(Galatians 5:14, NIV)

And over all these virtues put on love, which binds them all together in perfect unity.

(Colossians 3:14, NIV)

If you really keep the royal law found in Scripture, "Love your neighbor as yourself," you are doing right.

(James 2:8, NIV)

We know that we have passed from death to life, because we love the brethren. He who does not love his brother abides in death.

(1 John 3:14, NKJV)

By this we know that we love the children of God, when we love God and keep His commandments.

(1 John 5:2, NKJV)

Lust

Let not sin therefore rule as king in your mortal (short-lived, perishable) bodies, to make you yield to its cravings and be subject to its lusts and evil passions. For sin shall not [any longer] exert dominion over you, since now you are not under Law [as slaves], but under grace [as subjects of God's favor and mercy].

(Romans 6:12, 14, AMP)

So I say, live by the Spirit, and you will not gratify the desires of the sinful nature. For the sinful nature desires what is contrary to the Spirit, and the Spirit what is contrary to the sinful nature. They are in conflict with each other, so that you do not do what you want.

(Galatians 5:16–17, NIV)

Now those who belong to Christ Jesus have crucified the flesh with its passions and desires.

(Galatians 5:24, NASB)

Among them we too all formerly lived in the lusts of our flesh, indulging the desires of the flesh and of the mind, and were by nature children of wrath, even as the rest. But God, being rich in mercy, because of His great love with which He loved us, even when we were dead in our transgressions, made us alive together with Christ (by grace you have been saved).

(Ephesians 2:3–5, NASB)

For this is the will of God, that you should be consecrated (separated and set apart for pure and holy living): that you should abstain and shrink from all sexual vice, that each one of you should know how to possess (control, manage) his own body in consecration (purity, separated from things profane) and honor, not [to be used] in the passion of lust like the heathen, who are ignorant of the true God and have no knowledge of His will.

(1 Thessalonians 4:3–5, AMP)

For the grace of God that brings salvation has appeared to all men. It teaches us to say "No" to ungodliness and worldly passions, and to live self-controlled, upright and godly lives in this present age.

(Titus 2:11–12, NIV)

For we also once were foolish ourselves, disobedient, deceived, enslaved to various lusts and pleasures, spending our life in malice and envy, hateful, hating one another. But when the kindness of God our Savior and His love for mankind appeared, He saved us, not on the basis of deeds which we have done in righteousness, but according to His mercy.

(Titus 3:3–5a, NASB)

As obedient children, do not be conformed to the former lusts which were yours in your ignorance, but like the Holy One who called you, be holy yourselves also in all your behavior; because it is written, "You shall be holy, for I am holy."

(1 Peter 1:14–16, NASB)

Beloved, I implore you as aliens and strangers and exiles [in this world] to abstain from the sensual urges (the evil desires, the passions of the flesh, your lower nature) that wage war against the soul.

(1 Peter 2:11, AMP)

For everything in the world—the cravings of sinful man, the lust of his eyes and the boasting of what he has and does—comes not from the Father but from the world. The world and its desires pass away, but the man who does the will of God lives forever.

(1 John 2:16–17, NIV)

Lying

Whoever of you loves life and desires to see many good days, keep your tongue from evil and your lips from speaking lies.

(Psalm 34:12–13, NIV)

Truthful lips shall be established forever, but a lying tongue is [credited] but for a moment.

(Proverbs 12:19, AMP)

Lying lips are extremely disgusting and hateful to the Lord, but they who deal faithfully are His delight.

(Proverbs 12:22, AMP)

A false witness will not go unpunished, and he who speaks lies will not escape.

(Proverbs 19:5, NKJV)

That which is desired in a man is loyalty and kindness [and his glory and delight are his giving], but a poor man is better than a liar.

(Proverbs 19:22, AMP)

Do not lie to one another, since you laid aside the old self with its evil practices, and have put on the new self who is being renewed to a true knowledge according to the image of the One who created him.

(Colossians 3:9–10, NASB)

But the cowardly, the unbelieving, the vile, the murderers, the sexually immoral, those who practice magic arts, the idolaters and all liars—their place will be in the fiery lake of burning sulfur. This is the second death.

(Revelation 21:8, NIV)

Money

But you shall remember the Lord your God, for it is He who is giving you power to make wealth.

(Deuteronomy 8:18a, NASB)

A little that a righteous man has is better than the riches of many wicked.

(Psalm 37:16, NKJV)

But man, despite his riches, does not endure; he is like the beasts that perish. Their forms will decay in the grave, far from their princely mansions. But God will redeem my life from the grave; he will surely take me to himself.

(Psalm 49:12; 14c-15, NIV)

Turn my heart toward your statutes and not toward selfish gain.

(Psalm 119:36, NIV)

Wealth is worthless in the day of wrath, but righteousness delivers from death.

(Proverbs 11:4, NIV)

He who trusts in his riches will fall, but the righteous will flourish like the green leaf.

(Proverbs 11:28, NASB)

Wealth obtained by fraud dwindles, but the one who gathers by labor increases it.

(Proverbs 13:11, NASB)

Better is a little with the fear of the Lord, than great treasure with trouble.

(Proverbs 15:16, NKJV)

The rich man's wealth is his strong city, and as a high protecting wall in his own imagination and conceit.

(Proverbs 18:11, Amp)

Do not wear yourself out to get rich; have the wisdom to show restraint. Cast but a glance at riches, and they are gone, for they will surely sprout wings and fly off to the sky like an eagle.

(Proverbs 23:4–5, niv)

Better is the poor man who walks in his integrity than he who willfully goes in double and wrong ways, though he is rich.

(Proverbs 28:6, Amp)

A faithful man will abound with blessings, but he who makes haste to be rich will not go unpunished.

(Proverbs 28:20, nasb)

There is a serious and severe evil which I have seen under the sun: riches were kept by their owner to his hurt. But those riches are lost in a bad venture; and he becomes the father of a son, and there is nothing in his hand [with which to support the child]. As [the man] came forth from his mother's womb, so he will go again, naked as he came; and he will take away nothing for all his labor which he can carry in his hand.

(Ecclesiastes 5:13–15, Amp)

Moreover, when God gives any man wealth and possessions, and enables him to enjoy them, to accept his lot and be happy in his work—this is a gift of God. He seldom reflects on the days of his life, because God keeps him occupied with gladness of heart.

(Ecclesiastes 5:19–20, NIV)

Do not lay up for yourselves treasures on earth, where moth and rust destroy and where thieves break in and steal; but lay up for yourselves treasures in heaven, where neither moth nor rust destroys and where thieves do not break in and steal. For where your treasure is, there your heart will be also.

(Matthew 6:19–21, NKJV)

And the disciples were astonished at His words. But Jesus answered again and said to them, "Children, how hard it is for those who trust in riches to enter the kingdom of God! It is easier for a camel to go through the eye of a needle than for a rich man to enter the kingdom of God."

(Mark 10:24–25, NKJV)

I tell you, use worldly wealth to gain friends for yourselves, so that when it is gone, you will be welcomed into eternal dwellings.

(Luke 16:9, NIV)

And God is able to make all grace (every favor and earthly blessing) come to you in abundance, so that you may always and under all circumstances and whatever the need be self-sufficient [possessing enough to require no aid or support and furnished in abundance for every good work and charitable donation].

(2 Corinthians 9:8, AMP)

And constant friction between men of corrupt mind, who have been robbed of the truth and who think that godliness is a means to financial gain. But godliness with contentment is great gain.

(1 Timothy 6:5–6, NIV)

But those who want to get rich fall into temptation and a snare and many foolish and harmful desires which plunge men into ruin and destruction. For the love of money is a root of all sorts of evil, and some by longing for it have wandered away from the faith and pierced themselves with many griefs.

(1 Timothy 6:9–10, NASB)

For you say, I am rich; I have prospered and grown wealthy, and I am in need of nothing; and you do not realize and understand that you are wretched, pitiable, poor, blind, and naked.

(Revelation 3:17, AMP)

New Life

I will give you a new heart and put a new spirit within you; I will take the heart of stone out of your flesh and give you a heart of flesh.

(Ezekiel 36:26, NKJV)

Therefore we have been buried with Him through baptism into death, so that as Christ was raised from the dead through the glory of the Father, so we too might walk in newness of life. For if we have become united with Him in the likeness of His death, certainly we shall also be in the likeness of His resurrection, knowing this, that our old self was crucified with Him, in order that our body of sin might be done away with, so that we would no longer be slaves to sin; for he who has died is freed from sin.

(Romans 6:4–7, NASB)

Do you not know that your body is a temple of the Holy Spirit, who is in you, whom you have received from God? You are not your own; you were bought at a price. Therefore honor God with your body.

(1 Corinthians 6:19–20, NIV)

Therefore, if anyone is in Christ, he is a new creation; old things have passed away; behold, all things have become new.

(2 Corinthians 5:17, NKJV)

You were taught, with regard to your former way of life, to put off your old self, which is being corrupted by its deceitful desires; to be made new in the attitude of your minds; and to put on the new self, created to be like God in true righteousness and holiness.

(Ephesians 4:22–24, NIV)

But when the kindness and love of God our Savior appeared, he saved us, not because of righteous things we had done, but because of his mercy. He saved us through the washing of rebirth and renewal by the Holy Spirit.

(Titus 3:4–5, NIV)

Blessed be the God and Father of our Lord Jesus Christ, who according to His great mercy has caused us to be born again to a living hope through the resurrection of Jesus Christ from the dead, to obtain an inheritance which is imperishable and undefiled and will not fade away, reserved in heaven for you.

(1 Peter 1:3–4, NASB)

For you have been born again not of seed which is perishable but imperishable, that is, through the living and enduring word of God.

(1 Peter 1:23, NASB)

Obedience

You have commanded us to keep Your precepts, that we should observe them diligently.

(Psalm 119:4, AMP)

He who turns away his ear from hearing the law [of God and man], even his prayer is an abomination, hateful and revolting [to God].

(Proverbs 28:9, AMP)

Not everyone who says to me, "Lord, Lord," will enter the kingdom of heaven, but only he who does the will of my Father who is in heaven.

(Matthew 7:21, NIV)

Most assuredly, I say to you, if anyone keeps My word he shall never see death.

(John 8:51, NKJV)

If you know these things, blessed are you if you do them.

(John 13:17, NKJV)

Anyone who does not [really] love Me does not observe and obey My teaching. And the teaching which you hear and heed is not Mine, but [comes] from the Father Who sent Me.

(John 14:24, AMP)

If you keep My commandments [if you continue to obey My instructions], you will abide in My love and live on in it, just as I have obeyed My Father's commandments and live on in His love.

(John 15:10, AMP)

For it is not those who hear the law who are righteous in God's sight, but it is those who obey the law who will be declared righteous.

(Romans 2:13, NIV)

By this we know that we have come to know Him, if we keep His commandments. The one who says, "I have come to know Him," and does not keep His commandments, is a liar, and the truth is not in him; but whoever keeps His word, in him the love of God has truly been perfected.

(1 John 2:3–5a, NASB)

Occult
(see Superstition)

Paradise
(see also Eternal Life and Judgment)

So it was that the beggar died, and was carried by the angels to Abraham's bosom. The rich man also died and was buried. And being in torments in Hades, he lifted up his eyes and saw Abraham afar off, and Lazarus in his bosom. Then he cried and said, "Father Abraham, have mercy on me, and send Lazarus that he may dip the tip of his finger in water and cool my tongue; for I am tormented in this flame."

But Abraham said, "Son, remember that in your lifetime you received your good things, and likewise Lazarus evil things; but now he is comforted and you are tormented. And besides all this, between us and you there is a great gulf fixed, so that those who want to pass from here to you cannot, nor can those from there pass to us."

(Luke 16:22–26, NKJV)

And He answered him, Truly I tell you, today you shall be with Me in Paradise.

(Luke 23:43, AMP)

I know a man in Christ who fourteen years ago—whether in the body I do not know, or out of the body I do not know, God knows—such a man was caught up to the third heaven. And I know how such a man—whether in the body or apart from the body I do not know, God

knows—was caught up into Paradise and heard inexpressible words, which a man is not permitted to speak.

(2 Corinthians 12:2–4, NASB)

Therefore, since we have a great high priest who has gone
through the heavens, Jesus the Son of God, let us hold
firmly to the faith we profess.

(Hebrews 4:14, NIV)

He who has an ear, let him hear what the Spirit says to
the churches. To him who overcomes I will give to eat
from the tree of life, which is in the midst of the Paradise
of God.

(Revelation 2:7, NKJV)

Parenting
(see also Family)

You shall love the Lord your God with all your heart,
with all your soul, and with all your strength. And these
words which I command you today shall be in your heart.
You shall teach them diligently to your children, and shall
talk of them when you sit in your house, when you walk
by the way, when you lie down, and when you rise up.

(Deuteronomy 6:5–7, NKJV)

He who spares his rod hates his son, but he who loves
him disciplines him promptly.

(Proverbs 13:24, NKJV)

Discipline your son while there is hope, and do not desire his death.

(Proverbs 19:18, NASB)

Train up a child in the way he should go, and when he is old he will not depart from it.

(Proverbs 22:6, NKJV)

The rod and rebuke give wisdom, but a child left to himself brings shame to his mother. Correct your son, and he will give you rest; yes, he will give delight to your soul.

(Proverbs 29:15, 17, NKJV)

For children are not responsible to save up for their parents, but parents for their children.

(2 Corinthians 12:14b, NASB)

And you, fathers, do not provoke your children to wrath, but bring them up in the training and admonition of the Lord.

(Ephesians 6:4, NKJV)

Fathers, do not provoke your children, lest they become discouraged.

(Colossians 3:21, NKJV)

Patience

Wait on the Lord; be of good courage, and he shall strengthen your heart; wait, I say, on the Lord!

(Psalm 27:14, NKJV)

A fool's wrath is quickly and openly known, but a prudent man ignores an insult.

(Proverbs 12:16, AMP)

The end of a thing is better than its beginning; the patient in spirit is better than the proud in spirit.

(Ecclesiastes 7:8, NKJV)

And not only that, but we also glory in tribulations, knowing that tribulation produces perseverance; and perseverance, character; and character, hope.

(Romans 5:3–4, NKJV)

And we urge you, brothers, warn those who are idle, encourage the timid, help the weak, be patient with everyone.

(1 Thessalonians 5:14, NIV)

Consider it pure joy, my brothers, whenever you face trials of many kinds, because you know that the testing of your faith develops perseverance. Perseverance must finish its work so that you may be mature and complete, not lacking anything.

(James 1:2–4, NIV)

Peace, Inner
(see also Contentment)

Mark the blameless man and behold the upright, for there is a happy end for the man of peace.

(Psalm 37:37, AMP)

You will keep in perfect peace him whose mind is steadfast, because he trusts in you.

(Isaiah 26:3, NIV)

The work of righteousness will be peace, and the effect of righteousness, quietness and assurance forever.

(Isaiah 32:17, NKJV)

But the wicked are like the troubled sea, when it cannot rest, whose waters cast up mire and dirt. "There is no peace," says my God, "for the wicked."

(Isaiah 57:20–21, NKJV)

Come to me, all you who are weary and burdened, and I will give you rest. Take my yoke upon you and learn from me, for I am gentle and humble in heart, and you will find rest for your souls. For my yoke is easy and my burden is light.

(Matthew 11:28–30, NIV)

Peace I leave with you, My peace I give to you; not as the world gives do I give to you. Let not your heart be troubled, neither let it be afraid.

(John 14:27, NKJV)

For the kingdom of God is not eating and drinking, but righteousness and peace and joy in the Holy Spirit. For he who serves Christ in these things is acceptable to God and approved by men. Therefore let us pursue the things which make for peace and the things by which one may edify another.

(Romans 14:17–19, NKJV)

For God is not a God of confusion but of peace.

(1 Corinthians 14:33a, NASB)

Pleasure, Worldly

I said to myself, "Come now, I will test you with pleasure. So enjoy yourself." And behold, it too was futility. All that my eyes desired I did not refuse them. I did not withhold my heart from any pleasure, for my heart was pleased because of all my labor and this was my reward for all my labor. Thus I considered all my activities which my hands had done and the labor which I had exerted, and behold all was vanity and striving after wind and there was no profit under the sun.

(Ecclesiastes 2:1; 10–11, NASB)

The seed which fell among the thorns, these are the ones who have heard, and as they go on their way they are choked with worries and riches and pleasures of this life, and bring no fruit to maturity.

(Luke 8:14, NASB)

Prayer

If I had cherished sin in my heart, the Lord would not have listened; but God has surely listened and heard my voice in prayer.

(Psalm 66:18–19, NIV)

The Lord is far from the wicked, but He hears the prayer of the righteous.

(Proverbs 15:29, NKJV)

And when you pray, you shall not be like the hypocrites. For they love to pray standing in the synagogues and on the corners of the streets, that they may be seen by men. Assuredly, I say to you, they have their reward. But you, when you pray, go into your room, and when you have shut your door, pray to your Father who is in the secret place; and your Father who sees in secret will reward you openly. And when you pray, do not use vain repetitions as the heathen do. For they think that they will be heard for their many words. Therefore do not be like them. For your Father knows the things you have need of before you ask Him.

(Matthew 6:5–8, NKJV)

Ask, and it will be given to you; seek, and you will find; knock, and it will be opened to you. For everyone who asks receives, and he who seeks finds, and to him who knocks it will be opened.

(Matthew 7:7–8, NKJV)

If you then, being evil, know how to give good gifts to your children, how much more will your Father who is in heaven give good things to those who ask Him!

(Matthew 7:11, NKJV)

And whatever you ask for in prayer, having faith and [really] believing, you will receive.

(Matthew 21:22, AMP)

Then He spoke a parable to them, that men always ought to pray and not lose heart.

(Luke 18:1, NKJV)

We know that God does not listen to sinners. He listens to the godly man who does his will.

(John 9:31, NIV)

Peter was therefore kept in prison, but constant prayer was offered to God for him by the church.

(Acts 12:5, NKJV)

In the same way, the Spirit helps us in our weakness. We do not know what we ought to pray for, but the Spirit himself intercedes for us with groans that words cannot express.

(Romans 8:26, NIV)

Be joyful always; pray continually; give thanks in all circumstances, for this is God's will for you in Christ Jesus.

(1 Thessalonians 5:16–18, NIV)

When you ask, you do not receive, because you ask with wrong motives, that you may spend what you get on your pleasures.

(James 4:3, NIV)

Confess your trespasses to one another, and pray for one another, that you may be healed. The effective, fervent prayer of a righteous man avails much.

(James 5:16, NKJV)

For the eyes of the Lord are on the righteous, and His ears are open to their prayers; but the face of the Lord is against those who do evil.

(1 Peter 3:12, NKJV)

This is the confidence we have in approaching God: that if we ask anything according to his will, he hears us. And if we know that he hears us—whatever we ask—we know that we have what we asked of him.

(1 John 5:14–15, NIV)

Prejudice

For the Lord does not see as man sees; for man looks at the outward appearance, but the Lord looks at the heart.

(1 Samuel 16:7b, NKJV)

The Lord looks from heaven, He beholds all the sons of men; from His dwelling place He looks [intently] upon all the inhabitants of the earth—He Who fashions the hearts of them all, Who considers all their doings.

(Psalm 33:13–15, AMP)

Jesus left there and went to his hometown, accompanied by his disciples. When the Sabbath came, he began to teach in the synagogue, and many who heard him were amazed."Where did this man get these things?" they asked. "What's this wisdom that has been given him, that he even does miracles! Isn't this the carpenter? Isn't this Mary's son and the brother of James, Joseph, Judas and

Simon? Aren't his sisters here with us?" And they took offense at him.

Jesus said to them, "Only in his hometown, among his relatives and in his own house is a prophet without honor."

(Mark 6:1–4, NIV)

Philip found Nathanael and said to him, "We have found Him of whom Moses in the law, and also the prophets, wrote—Jesus of Nazareth, the son of Joseph." And Nathanael said to him, "Can anything good come out of Nazareth?" Philip said to him, "Come and see."

(John 1:45–46, NKJV)

Then he said to them, "You know how unlawful it is for a Jewish man to keep company with or go to one of another nation. But God has shown me that I should not call any man common or unclean."

(Acts 10:28, NKJV)

Opening his mouth, Peter said: "I most certainly understand now that God is not one to show partiality, but in every nation the man who fears Him and does what is right is welcome to Him."

(Acts 10:34–35, NASB)

There is neither Jew nor Greek, there is neither slave nor free, there is neither male nor female; for you are all one in Christ Jesus.

(Galatians 3:28, NKJV)

With good will render service, as to the Lord, and not to men, knowing that whatever good thing each one does, this he will receive back from the Lord, whether slave or free.

(Ephesians 6:7–8, NASB)

I charge you before God and the Lord Jesus Christ and the elect angels that you observe these things without prejudice, doing nothing with partiality.

(1 Timothy 5:21, NKJV)

My brethren, do not hold the faith of our Lord Jesus Christ, the Lord of glory, with partiality. For if there should come into your assembly a man with gold rings, in fine apparel, and there should also come in a poor man in filthy clothes, and you pay attention to the one wearing the fine clothes and say to him, "You sit here in a good place," and say to the poor man, "You stand there," or, "Sit here at my footstool," have you not shown partiality among yourselves, and become judges with evil thoughts?

(James 2:1–4, NKJV)

If you really keep the royal law found in Scripture, "Love your neighbor as yourself," you are doing right. But if you show favoritism, you sin and are convicted by the law as lawbreakers.

(James 2:8–9, NIV)

But the wisdom that comes from heaven is first of all pure; then peace-loving, considerate, submissive, full of mercy and good fruit, impartial and sincere.

(James 3:17, NIV)

If you address as Father the One who impartially judges according to each one's work, conduct yourselves in fear during the time of your stay on earth.

(1 Peter 1:17, NASB)

Pretentiousness
(see also Hypocrisy)

Better to be a nobody and yet have a servant than pretend to be somebody and have no food.

(Proverbs 12:9, NIV)

The wisdom of the sensible is to understand his way, but the foolishness of fools is deceit.

(Proverbs 14:8, NASB)

And when you pray, do not be like the hypocrites, for they love to pray standing in the synagogues and on the street corners to be seen by men. I tell you the truth, they have received their reward in full.

(Matthew 6:5, NIV)

Pride

(see also Arrogance and Conceit)

In his pride the wicked does not seek him; in all his thoughts there is no room for God.

(Psalm 10:4, NIV)

Whoever secretly slanders his neighbor, him I will destroy; the one who has a haughty look and a proud heart, him I will not endure.

(Psalm 101:5, NKJV)

O Lord, my heart is not proud, nor my eyes haughty; nor do I involve myself in great matters, or in things too difficult for me. Surely I have composed and quieted my soul; like a weaned child rests against his mother, my soul is like a weaned child within me.

(Psalm 131:1–2, NASB)

These six things the Lord hates, yes, seven are an abomination to Him: a proud look, a lying tongue, hands that shed innocent blood, a heart that devises wicked plans, feet that are swift in running to evil, a false witness who speaks lies, and one who sows discord among brethren.

(Proverbs 6:16–19, NKJV)

Pride only breeds quarrels, but wisdom is found in those who take advice.

(Proverbs 13:10, NIV)

Pride goes before destruction, and a haughty spirit before a fall.

(Proverbs 16:18, NKJV)

Haughty eyes and a proud heart, the lamp of the wicked, are sin!

(Proverbs 21:4, NIV)

Do you see a man wise in his own eyes? There is more hope for a fool than for him.

(Proverbs 26:12, NKJV)

How can you believe, when you receive glory from one another and you do not seek the glory that is from the one and only God?

(John 5:44, NASB)

But, "Let him who boasts boast in the Lord." For it is not the one who commends himself who is approved, but the one whom the Lord commends.

(2 Corinthians 10:17–18, NIV)

Procrastination

Do not boast about tomorrow, for you do not know what a day may bring forth.

(Proverbs 27:1, NKJV)

Now as he reasoned about righteousness, self-control, and the judgment to come, Felix was afraid and answered,

"Go away for now; when I have a convenient time I will call for you."

(Acts 24:25, NKJV)

Quarrelling
(see Arguing)

Relationships
(see also Loving Others)

How good and pleasant it is when brothers live together in unity.

(Psalm 133:1, NIV)

Anxiety in a man's heart weighs it down, but an encouraging word makes it glad.

(Proverbs 12:25, AMP)

A man has joy in an apt answer, and how delightful is a timely word!

(Proverbs 15:23, NASB)

He who covers and forgives an offense seeks love, but he who repeats or harps on a matter separates even close friends.

(Proverbs 17:9, AMP)

A man's wisdom gives him patience; it is to his glory to overlook an offense.

(Proverbs 19:11, NIV)

A word fitly spoken is like apples of gold in settings of silver.

(Proverbs 25:11, NKJV)

As iron sharpens iron, so one man sharpens another.

(Proverbs 27:17, NIV)

So in everything, do to others what you would have them do to you, for this sums up the Law and the Prophets.

(Matthew 7:12, NIV)

Rejoice with those who rejoice; mourn with those who mourn. Live in harmony with one another. Do not be proud, but be willing to associate with people of low position. Do not be conceited.

(Romans 12:15–16, NIV)

If possible, as far as it depends on you, live at peace with everyone.

(Romans 12:18, AMP)

Give everyone what you owe him: If you owe taxes, pay taxes; if revenue, then revenue; if respect, then respect; if honor, then honor.

(Romans 13:7–8, NIV)

Therefore, accept one another, just as Christ also accepted us to the glory of God.

(Romans 15:7, NASB)

Do not be yoked together with unbelievers. For what do

righteousness and wickedness have in common? Or what fellowship can light have with darkness?

(2 Corinthians 6:14, NIV)

If you keep on biting and devouring each other, watch out or you will be destroyed by each other.

(Galatians 5:15, NIV)

With all humility and gentleness, with patience, showing tolerance for one another in love, being diligent to preserve the unity of the Spirit in the bond of peace.

(Ephesians 4:2–3, NASB)

Do not let any unwholesome talk come out of your mouths, but only what is helpful for building others up according to their needs, that it may benefit those who listen.

(Ephesians 4:29, NIV)

Be wise in the way you act toward outsiders; make the most of every opportunity. Let your conversation be always full of grace, seasoned with salt, so that you may know how to answer everyone.

(Colossians 4:5–6, NIV)

Since you have in obedience to the truth purified your souls for a sincere love of the brethren, fervently love one another from the heart.

(1 Peter 1:22, NASB)

Repentance
(see also Believing and Salvation)

I considered my ways; I turned my feet to [obey] Your testimonies.

(Psalm 119:59, Amp)

And Jesus answered and said to them, "It is not those who are well who need a physician, but those who are sick. I have not come to call the righteous but sinners to repentance."

(Luke 5:31–32, nasb)

I say to you that likewise there will be more joy in heaven over one sinner who repents than over ninety-nine just persons who need no repentance.

(Luke 15:7, nkjv)

Peter replied, "Repent and be baptized, every one of you, in the name of Jesus Christ for the forgiveness of your sins. And you will receive the gift of the Holy Spirit."

(Acts 2:38, niv)

Repent therefore and be converted, that your sins may be blotted out, so that times of refreshing may come from the presence of the Lord.

(Acts 3:19, nkjv)

Truly, these times of ignorance God overlooked, but now commands all men everywhere to repent.

(Acts 17:30, nkjv)

Or do you think lightly of the riches of His kindness and tolerance and patience, not knowing that the kindness of God leads you to repentance?

(Romans 2:4, NASB)

The Lord is not slack concerning His promise, as some count slackness, but is longsuffering toward us, not willing that any should perish but that all should come to repentance.

(2 Peter 3:9, NKJV)

Those whom I love I rebuke and discipline. So be earnest, and repent.

(Revelation 3:19, NIV)

Reputation

Let love and faithfulness never leave you; bind them around your neck, write them on the tablet of your heart. Then you will win favor and a good name in the sight of God and man.

(Proverbs 3:3–4, NIV)

A good name is more desirable than great riches; to be esteemed is better than silver or gold. Rich and poor have this in common: The Lord is the Maker of them all.

(Proverbs 22:1–2, NIV)

A good name is better than precious perfume.

(Ecclesiastes 7:1a, AMP)

Respect

Rise in the presence of the aged, show respect for the elderly and revere your God. I am the Lord.

(Leviticus 19:32, NIV)

Do nothing out of selfish ambition or vain conceit, but in humility consider others better than yourselves.

(Philippians 2:3, NIV)

Do not rebuke an older man harshly, but exhort him as if he were your father. Treat younger men as brothers, older women as mothers, and younger women as sisters, with absolute purity.

(1 Timothy 5:1–2, NIV)

Show proper respect to everyone: Love the brotherhood of believers, fear God, honor the king.

(1 Peter 2:17, NIV)

Young men, in the same way be submissive to those who are older.

(1 Peter 5:5a, NIV)

Resurrection
(see Eternal Life)

Revenge

You shall not take revenge or bear any grudge against the

sons of your people, but you shall love your neighbor as yourself. I am the Lord.

(Leviticus 19:18, AMP)

He who returns evil for good, evil will not depart from his house.

(Proverbs 17:13, NASB)

Say not, I will do to him as he has done to me; I will pay the man back for his deed.

(Proverbs 24:29, AMP)

You have heard that it was said, "An eye for an eye and a tooth for a tooth." But I tell you not to resist an evil person. But whoever slaps you on your right cheek, turn the other to him also.

(Matthew 5:38–39, NKJV)

Never pay back evil for evil to anyone. Respect what is right in the sight of all men. Never take your own revenge, beloved, but leave room for the wrath of God, for it is written, "Vengeance is Mine, I will repay," says the Lord.

(Romans 12:17, 19, NASB)

See that none of you repays another with evil for evil, but always aim to show kindness and seek to do good to one another and to everybody.

(1 Thessalonians 5:15, AMP)

When they hurled their insults at him, he did not retaliate; when he suffered, he made no threats. Instead, he entrusted himself to him who judges justly.

(1 Peter 2:23, NIV)

Do not repay evil with evil or insult with insult, but with blessing, because to this you were called so that you may inherit a blessing.

(1 Peter 3:9, NIV)

Riches
(see Money)

Righteousness
(see also Character)

For You, O Lord, will bless the righteous; with favor You will surround him as with a shield.

(Psalm 5:12, NKJV)

I have been young and now I am old, yet I have not seen the righteous forsaken or his descendants begging bread.

(Psalm 37:25, NASB)

How can a young man keep his way pure? By keeping it according to Your word.

(Psalm 119:9, NASB)

The path of the righteous is like the first gleam of dawn, shining ever brighter till the full light of day.

(Proverbs 4:18, NIV)

The wages of the righteous bring them life, but the income of the wicked brings them punishment.

(Proverbs 10:16, NIV)

The righteousness of the upright delivers them, but the unfaithful are trapped by evil desires.

(Proverbs 11:6, NIV)

Adversity pursues sinners, but the righteous will be rewarded with prosperity.

(Proverbs 13:21, NASB)

The wicked flee when no one pursues, but the righteous are bold as a lion.

(Proverbs 28:1, NKJV)

Although a wicked man commits a hundred crimes and still lives a long time, I know that it will go better with God-fearing men, who are reverent before God.

(Ecclesiastes 8:12, NIV)

Say to the righteous that it shall be well with them, for they shall eat the fruit of their deeds.

(Isaiah 3:10, AMP)

Blessed are those who hunger and thirst for righteousness, for they shall be filled.

(Matthew 5:6, NKJV)

The good man brings good things out of the good stored

up in him, and the evil man brings evil things out of the evil stored up in him.

(Matthew 12:35, NIV)

I put this in human terms because you are weak in your natural selves. Just as you used to offer the parts of your body in slavery to impurity and to ever-increasing wickedness, so now offer them in slavery to righteousness leading to holiness. When you were slaves to sin, you were free from the control of righteousness. What benefit did you reap at that time from the things you are now ashamed of? Those things result in death! But now that you have been set free from sin and have become slaves to God, the benefit you reap leads to holiness and the result is eternal life.

(Romans 6:19–22, NIV)

If Christ is in you, though the body is dead because of sin, yet the spirit is alive because of righteousness.

(Romans 8:10, NASB)

Sacrifice
(see Self-Denial)

Salvation
(see also Believing and Repentance)

Behold, the Lord's hand is not so short that it cannot save; nor is His ear so dull that it cannot hear. But your iniquities have made a separation between you and your

God, and your sins have hidden His face from you so that
He does not hear.

(Isaiah 59:1–2, NASB)

Say to them, As I live, says the Lord God, I have no
pleasure in the death of the wicked, but rather that the
wicked turn from his way and live.

(Ezekiel 33:11a, AMP)

For the Son of Man has come to seek and to save that
which was lost.

(Luke 19:10, NKJV)

For God did not send His Son into the world to condemn the world, but that the world through Him might
be saved.

(John 3:17, NKJV)

And other sheep I have which are not of this fold; them
also I must bring, and they will hear My voice; and there
will be one flock and one shepherd.

(John 10:16, NKJV)

And there is salvation in no one else; for there is no other
name under heaven that has been given among men by
which we must be saved.

(Acts 4:12, NASB)

That if you confess with your mouth Jesus as Lord, and
believe in your heart that God raised Him from the dead,
you will be saved; for with the heart a person believes,

resulting in righteousness, and with the mouth he confesses, resulting in salvation.

(Romans 10:9–10, NASB)

By this gospel you are saved, if you hold firmly to the word I preached to you. Otherwise, you have believed in vain.

(1 Corinthians 15:2, NIV)

Therefore, my beloved, as you have always obeyed, not as in my presence only, but now much more in my absence, work out your own salvation with fear and trembling.

(Philippians 2:12, NKJV)

For God has not destined us for wrath, but for obtaining salvation through our Lord Jesus Christ.

(1 Thessalonians 5:9, NASB)

This is a faithful saying and worthy of all acceptance, that Christ Jesus came into the world to save sinners, of whom I am chief.

(1 Timothy 1:15, NKJV)

This is good and acceptable in the sight of God our Savior, who desires all men to be saved and to come to the knowledge of the truth. For there is one God, and one mediator also between God and men, the man Christ Jesus, who gave Himself as a ransom for all, the testimony given at the proper time.

(1 Timothy 2:3–6, NASB)

Who gave himself for us to redeem us from all wickedness and to purify for himself a people that are his very own, eager to do what is good.

(Titus 2:14, NIV)

But Jesus, on the other hand, because He continues forever, holds His priesthood permanently. Therefore He is able also to save forever those who draw near to God through Him, since He always lives to make intercession for them.

(Hebrews 7:24–25, NASB)

Like newborn babies, crave pure spiritual milk, so that by it you may grow up in your salvation, now that you have tasted that the Lord is good.

(1 Peter 2:2–3, NIV)

Second Coming
(see Judgment)

Security
(see Confidence)

Self-Control
(see also Speech, Careless)

Like a city whose walls are broken down is a man who lacks self-control.

(Proverbs 25:28, NIV)

And we take captive every thought to make it obedient to Christ.

(2 Corinthians 10:5b, NIV)

For the grace of God that brings salvation has appeared to all men. It teaches us to say "No" to ungodliness and worldly passions, and to live self-controlled, upright and godly lives in this present age.

(Titus 2:11–12, NIV)

Be self-controlled and alert. Your enemy the devil prowls around like a roaring lion looking for someone to devour. Resist him, standing firm in the faith, because you know that your brothers throughout the world are undergoing the same kind of sufferings.

(1 Peter 5:8–9, NIV)

Self-Denial

Then Jesus said to his disciples, "If anyone would come after me, he must deny himself and take up his cross and follow me. What good will it be for a man if he gains the whole world, yet forfeits his soul? Or what can a man give in exchange for his soul?"

(Matthew 16:24, 26, NIV)

Then He said to them all, "If anyone desires to come after Me, let him deny himself, and take up his cross daily, and follow Me."

(Luke 9:23, NKJV)

And He said to them, I say to you truly, there is no one who has left house or wife or brothers or parents or children for the sake of the kingdom of God who will not receive in return many times more in this world and, in the coming age, eternal life.

(Luke 18:29–30, Amp)

Greater love has no one than this, that he lay down his life for his friends.

(John 15:13, niv)

And all those who had believed were together and had all things in common; and they began selling their property and possessions and were sharing them with all, as anyone might have need.

(Acts 2:44–45, nasb)

All the believers were one in heart and mind. No one claimed that any of his possessions was his own, but they shared everything they had.

(Acts 4:32, niv)

Nobody should seek his own good, but the good of others.

(1 Corinthians 10:24, niv)

Let this mind be in you which was also in Christ Jesus, who, being in the form of God, did not consider it robbery to be equal with God, but made Himself of no reputation, taking the form of a bondservant, and coming in the likeness of men. And being found in appearance as a man, He humbled Himself and became obedient to the point of death, even the death of the cross.

(Philippians 2:5–8, NKJV)

But whatsoever things were gain to me, those things I have counted as loss for the sake of Christ. More than that, I count all things to be loss in view of the surpassing value of knowing Christ Jesus my Lord, for whom I have suffered the loss of all things, and count them but rubbish so that I may gain Christ.

(Philippians 3:7–8, NASB)

Self-Esteem

When I consider Your heavens, the work of Your fingers, the moon and the stars, which You have ordained, what is man that You are mindful of him, and the son of man that You visit him? For You have made him a little lower than the angels, and You have crowned him with glory and honor. You have made him to have dominion over the works of Your hands; You have put all things under his feet.

(Psalm 8:3–6, NKJV)

Self-Examination

In your anger do not sin; when you are on your beds, search your hearts and be silent.

(Psalm 4:4, NIV)

Let us examine our ways and test them, and let us return to the Lord.

(Lamentations 3:40, NIV)

So then whoever eats the bread or drinks the cup of the Lord in a way that is unworthy [of Him] will be guilty of [profaning and sinning against] the body and blood of the Lord. Let a man [thoroughly] examine himself, and [only when he has done] so should he eat of the bread and drink of the cup. For if we searchingly examined ourselves [detecting our shortcomings and recognizing our own condition], we should not be judged and penalty decreed [by the divine judgment].

(1 Corinthians 11:27–28; 31, AMP)

Test yourselves to see if you are in the faith; examine yourselves! Or do you not recognize this about yourselves, that Jesus Christ is in you—unless indeed you fail the test?

(2 Corinthians 13:5, NASB)

Each one should test his own actions. Then he can take pride in himself, without comparing himself to somebody else.

(Galatians 6:4, NIV)

Self-Righteousness

All the ways of a man are clean in his own sight, but the Lord weighs the motives.

(Proverbs 16:2, NASB)

Do not gloat when your enemy falls; when he stumbles, do not let your heart rejoice.

(Proverbs 24:17, NIV)

When they kept on questioning him, he straightened up and said to them, "If any one of you is without sin, let him be the first to throw a stone at her."

(John 8:7, NIV)

For not knowing about God's righteousness and seeking to establish their own, they did not subject themselves to the righteousness of God.

(Romans 10:3, NASB)

For by the grace given me I say to every one of you: Do not think of yourself more highly than you ought, but rather think of yourself with sober judgment, in accordance with the measure of faith God has given you.

(Romans 12:3, NIV)

But, "Let him who boasts boast in the Lord." For it is not the one who commends himself who is approved, but the one whom the Lord commends.

(2 Corinthians 10:17–18, NIV)

Selfishness
(see Greed)

Senior Citizens
(see Aging)

Sickness

Bless the Lord, O my soul, and forget none of His benefits; who pardons all your iniquities, who heals all your diseases.

(Psalm 103:2–3, NASB)

Do not be wise in your own eyes; fear the Lord and turn away from evil. It will be healing to your body and refreshment to your bones.

(Proverbs 3:7–8, NASB)

My son, give attention to my words; incline your ear to my sayings. For they are life to those who find them and health to all their body.

(Proverbs 4:20, 22, NASB)

Pleasant words are like a honeycomb, sweetness to the soul and health to the bones.

(Proverbs 16:24, NKJV)

You restored me to health and let me live. Surely it was for my benefit that I suffered such anguish.

(Isaiah 38:16b-17a, NIV)

Because of the surpassing greatness of the revelations, for this reason, to keep me from exalting myself, there was given me a thorn in the flesh, a messenger of Satan to torment me—to keep me from exalting myself! Concerning this I implored the Lord three times that it might leave me. And he has said to me, "My grace is sufficient for you, for power is perfected in weakness." Most gladly, therefore, I will rather boast about my weaknesses, so that the power of Christ may dwell in me. Therefore I am well content with weaknesses, with insults, with distresses, with persecutions, with difficulties, for Christ's sake; for when I am weak, then I am strong.

(2 Corinthians 12:7–10, NASB)

Sin

Forgive my hidden faults. Keep your servant also from willful sins; may they not rule over me.

(Psalm 19:12b-13a, NIV)

Wash me thoroughly from my iniquity and cleanse me from my sin. For I know my transgressions, and my sin is ever before me. Against You, You only, I have sinned and done what is evil in Your sight, so that You are justified when You speak and blameless when You judge.

(Psalm 51:2–4, NASB)

You have set our iniquities before You, our secret sins in the light of Your countenance.

(Psalm 90:8, NKJV)

He has not dealt with us according to our sins, nor punished us according to our iniquities. For as the heavens are high above the earth, so great is His mercy toward those who fear Him.

(Psalm 103:10–11, NKJV)

The way of a guilty man is crooked, but as for the pure, his conduct is upright.

(Proverbs 21:8, NASB)

He who conceals his transgressions will not prosper, but he who confesses and forsakes them will find compassion.

(Proverbs 28:13, NASB)

Indeed, there is not a righteous man on earth who continually does good and who never sins.

(Ecclesiastes 7:20, NASB)

Anyone who breaks one of the least of these commandments and teaches others to do the same will be called least in the kingdom of heaven, but whoever practices and teaches these commands will be called great in the kingdom of heaven.

(Matthew 5:19, NIV)

You have heard that it was said to those of old, "You shall not commit adultery." But I say to you that whoever looks at a woman to lust for her has already committed adultery with her in his heart.

(Matthew 5:27–28, NKJV)

And hearing this, Jesus said to them, "It is not those who are healthy who need a physician, but those who are sick; I did not come to call the righteous, but sinners.

(Mark 2:17, NASB)

This is the judgment, that the Light has come into the

world, and men loved the darkness rather than the Light, for their deeds were evil. For everyone who does evil hates the Light, and does not come to the Light for fear that his deeds will be exposed. But he who practices the truth comes to the Light, so that his deeds may be manifested as having been wrought in God.

(John 3:19–21, NASB)

For all have sinned and fall short of the glory of God.

(Romans 3:23, NKJV)

For the wages of sin is death, but the gift of God is eternal life in Christ Jesus our Lord.

(Romans 6:23, NIV)

So I find this law at work: When I want to do good, evil is right there with me. For in my inner being I delight in God's law; but I see another law at work in the members of my body, waging war against the law of my mind and making me a prisoner of the law of sin at work within my members. What a wretched man I am! Who will rescue me from this body of death? Thanks be to God—through Jesus Christ our Lord!

(Romans 7:21–25a, NIV)

For those who are according to the flesh and are controlled by its unholy desires set their minds on and pursue those things which gratify the flesh, but those who are according to the Spirit and are controlled by the desires of the Spirit set their minds on and seek those things which gratify the [Holy] Spirit. Now the mind of the flesh [which is sense and reason without the Holy Spirit] is death [death that comprises all the miseries arising from sin, both here and hereafter]. But the mind of the [Holy] Spirit is life and [soul] peace [both now and forever]. [That is] because the mind of the flesh [with its carnal thoughts and purposes] is hostile to God, for it does not submit itself to God's law; indeed it cannot. So then those who are living the life of the flesh [catering to the appetites and impulses of their carnal nature] cannot please or satisfy God, or be acceptable to Him.

(Romans 8:5–8, AMP)

For if you live according to the flesh you will die; but if by the Spirit you put to death the deeds of the body, you will live. For as many as are led by the Spirit of God, these are sons of God.

(Romans 8:13–14, NKJV)

Do not be overcome by evil, but overcome evil with good.

(Romans 12:21, NKJV)

They are darkened in their understanding and separated from the life of God because of the ignorance that is in them due to the hardening of their hearts. Having lost all sensitivity, they have given themselves over to sensuality so as to indulge in every kind of impurity, with a continual lust for more.

(Ephesians 4:18–19, NIV)

For he who does wrong will receive the consequences of the wrong which he has done, and that without partiality.

(Colossians 3:25, NASB)

But each one is tempted when, by his own evil desire, he is dragged away and enticed. Then, after desire has conceived, it gives birth to sin; and sin, when it is full-grown, gives birth to death.

(James 1:14–15, NIV)

Submit yourselves, then, to God. Resist the devil, and he will flee from you. Come near to God and he will come near to you.

(James 4:7–8, NIV)

If we say that we have fellowship with Him, and walk in darkness, we lie and do not practice the truth. But if we walk in the light as He is in the light, we have fellowship with one another, and the blood of Jesus Christ His Son cleanses us from all sin. If we say that we have no sin, we deceive ourselves, and the truth is not in us. If we confess our sins, He is faithful and just to forgive us our sins and to cleanse us from all unrighteousness. If we say that we have not sinned, we make Him a liar, and His word is not in us.

(1 John 1:6–10, NKJV)

Little children, make sure no one deceives you; the one who practices righteousness is righteous, just as He is righteous; the one who practices sin is of the devil; for the devil has sinned from the beginning. The Son of God appeared for this purpose, to destroy the works of the devil. No one who is born of God practices sin, because His seed abides in him; and he cannot sin, because he is born of God.

(1 John 3:7–9, NASB)

Sin, Rejoicing in

Do not gloat when your enemy falls; when he stumbles, do not let your heart rejoice, or the Lord will see and disapprove and turn his wrath away from him.

(Proverbs 24:17–18, NIV)

Though they are fully aware of God's righteous decree that those who do such things deserve to die, they not only do them themselves but approve and applaud others who practice them.

(Romans 1:32, AMP)

Love does not delight in evil but rejoices with the truth.

(1 Corinthians 13:6, NIV)

Slander
(see Hypocrisy and Judging Others)

Sorcery
(see Superstition)

Sorrow
(see also Depression and Loneliness)

Weeping may endure for a night, but joy comes in the morning.

(Psalm 30:5b, NKJV)

My soul is weary with sorrow; strengthen me according to your word.

(Psalm 119:28, NIV)

Those who sow in tears will reap with songs of joy. He who goes out weeping, carrying seed to sow, will return with songs of joy, carrying sheaves with him.

(Psalm 126:5–6, NIV)

To everything there is a season, a time for every purpose under heaven: a time to weep, and a time to laugh; a time to mourn, and a time to dance.

(Ecclesiastes 3:1, 4, NKJV)

Blessed are those who mourn, for they shall be comforted.

(Matthew 5:4, NKJV)

For the sorrow that is according to the will of God produces a repentance without regret, leading to salvation, but the sorrow of the world produces death.

(2 Corinthians 7:10, NASB)

Speech, Careless
(see also Anger and Gossip and Self-Control)

Put away from you false and dishonest speech, and willful and contrary talk put far from you.

(Proverbs 4:24, Amp)

When there are many words, transgression is unavoidable. But he who restrains his lips is wise.

(Proverbs 10:19, nasb)

An evil man is trapped by his sinful talk, but a righteous man escapes trouble.

(Proverbs 12:13, niv)

There are those who speak rashly, like the piercing of a sword, but the tongue of the wise brings healing.

(Proverbs 12:18, Amp)

He who guards his mouth keeps his life, but he who opens wide his lips comes to ruin.

(Proverbs 13:3, Amp)

He who has knowledge spares his words, and a man of understanding has a cool spirit. Even a fool when he holds his peace is considered wise; when he closes his lips he is esteemed a man of understanding.

(Proverbs 17:27–28, Amp)

It is better not to vow than to make a vow and not fulfill it.

(Ecclesiastes 5:5, niv)

For in many dreams and in many words there is emptiness.

(Ecclesiastes 5:7a, NASB)

But I say to you that for every idle word men may speak, they will give account of it in the day of judgment. For by your words you will be justified, and by your words you will be condemned.

(Matthew 12:36–37, NKJV)

But avoid worldly and empty chatter, for it will lead to further ungodliness.

(2 Timothy 2:16, NASB)

Stewardship
(see Giving and Generosity)

Strength

What strength do I have, that I should still hope? What prospects, that I should be patient? Do I have the strength of stone? Is my flesh bronze? Do I have any power to help myself, now that success has been driven from me? Teach me, and I will be quiet; show me where I have been wrong.

(Job 6:11–13; 24, NIV)

In the day when I cried out, you answered me, and made me bold with strength in my soul.

(Psalm 138:3, NKJV)

He gives power to the weak, and to those who have no might He increases strength. Even the youths shall faint and be weary, and the young men shall utterly fall, but those who wait on the Lord shall renew their strength; they shall mount up with wings like eagles, they shall run and not be weary, they shall walk and not faint.

(Isaiah 40:29–31, NKJV)

Abide in Me, and I in you. As the branch cannot bear fruit of itself, unless it abides in the vine, neither can you, unless you abide in Me. I am the vine, you are the branches. He who abides in Me, and I in him, bears much fruit; for without Me you can do nothing.

(John 15:4–5, NKJV)

For the foolishness of God is wiser than man's wisdom, and the weakness of God is stronger than man's strength.

(1 Corinthians 1:25, NIV)

Be on your guard; stand firm in the faith; be men of courage; be strong.

(1 Corinthians 16:13, NIV)

Now to Him who is able to do far more abundantly beyond all that we ask or think, according to the power that works within us, to Him be the glory in the church and in Christ Jesus to all generations forever and ever. Amen.

(Ephesians 3:20–21, NASB)

Now may our Lord Jesus Christ Himself and God our Father, Who loved us and gave us everlasting consolation and encouragement and well-founded hope through [His] grace (unmerited favor), comfort and encourage your hearts and strengthen them [make them steadfast and keep them unswerving] in every good work and word.

(2 Thessalonians 2:16–17, Amp)

He who is in you is greater than he who is in the world.

(1 John 4:4b, nkjv)

Stumbling Block

Therefore let us stop passing judgment on one another. Instead, make up your mind not to put any stumbling block or obstacle in your brother's way.

(Romans 14:13, niv)

Be careful, however, that the exercise of your freedom does not become a stumbling block to the weak.

(1 Corinthians 8:9, niv)

Suffering
(see Hardship and Sickness)

Superstition

I will set my face against the person who turns to mediums and spiritists to prostitute himself by following them, and I will cut him off from his people.

(Leviticus 20:6, NIV)

There shall not be found among you anyone who makes his son or his daughter pass through the fire, one who uses divination, one who practices witchcraft, or one who interprets omens, or a sorcerer, or one who casts a spell, or a medium, or a spiritist, or one who calls up the dead. For whoever does these things is detestable to the Lord.

(Deuteronomy 18:10–12a, NASB)

When they say to you, "Consult the mediums and the spiritists who whisper and mutter," should not a people consult their God? Should they consult the dead on behalf of the living?

(Isaiah 8:19, NASB)

You are wearied with your many counsels; let now the astrologers, those who prophesy by the stars, those who predict by the new moons, stand up and save you from what will come upon you.

(Isaiah 47:13, NASB)

"So I will come near to you for judgment. I will be quick to testify against sorcerers, adulterers and perjurers, against those who defraud laborers of their wages, who oppress the widows and the fatherless, and deprive aliens of justice, but do not fear me," says the Lord Almighty.

(Malachi 3:5, NIV)

Many also of those who were now believers came making full confession and thoroughly exposing their [former deceptive and evil] practices. And many of those who had practiced curious, magical arts collected their books and [throwing them, book after book, on the pile] burned them in the sight of everybody. When they counted the value of them, they found it amounted to 50,000 pieces of silver (about $9,300). Thus the Word of the Lord [concerning the attainment through Christ of eternal salvation in the kingdom of God] grew and spread and intensified, prevailing mightily.

(Acts 19:18–20, AMP)

Now the doings (practices) of the flesh are clear (obvious): they are immorality, impurity, indecency, idolatry, sorcery, enmity, strife, jealousy, anger (ill temper), selfishness, divisions (dissensions), party spirit (factions, sects with peculiar opinions, heresies), envy, drunkenness, carousing, and the like. I warn you beforehand, just as I did previously, that those who do such things shall not inherit the kingdom of God.

(Galatians 5:19–21, AMP)

As I urged you upon my departure for Macedonia, remain on at Ephesus so that you may instruct certain men not to teach strange doctrines, nor to pay attention to myths and endless genealogies, which give rise to mere speculation rather than furthering the administration of God which is by faith.

(1 Timothy 1:3–4, NASB)

Have nothing to do with godless myths and old wives' tales; rather, train yourself to be godly.

(1 Timothy 4:7, NIV)

But the cowardly, the unbelieving, the vile, the murderers, the sexually immoral, those who practice magic arts, the idolaters and all liars—their place will be in the fiery lake of burning sulfur. This is the second death.

(Revelation 21:8, NIV)

But outside are dogs and sorcerers and sexually immoral and murderers and idolaters, and whoever loves and practices a lie.

(Revelation 22:15, NKJV)

Talents

All who are gifted artisans among you shall come and make all that the Lord has commanded: the tabernacle, its tent, its covering, its clasps, its boards, its bars, its pillars, and its sockets; the garments of ministry, for ministering in the holy place.

(Exodus 35:10–11; 19a, NKJV)

From everyone who has been given much, much will be demanded; and from the one who has been entrusted with much, much more will be asked.

(Luke 12:48b, NIV)

We have different gifts, according to the grace given us. If a man's gift is prophesying, let him use it in proportion to his faith. If it is serving, let him serve; if it is teaching, let him teach; if it is encouraging, let him encourage; if it is contributing to the needs of others, let him give generously; if it is leadership, let him govern diligently; if it is showing mercy, let him do it cheerfully.

(Romans 12:6–8, NIV)

There are different kinds of gifts, but the same Spirit. There are different kinds of service, but the same Lord. There are different kinds of working, but the same God works all of them in all men.

(1 Corinthians 12:4–6, NIV)

Every good and perfect gift is from above, coming down from the Father of the heavenly lights, who does not change like shifting shadows.

(James 1:17, NIV)

Each one should use whatever gift he has received to serve others, faithfully administering God's grace in its various forms.

(1 Peter 4:10, NIV)

Temper
(see Anger and Self-Control and Speech, Careless)

Temptation

My son, if sinners entice you, do not consent. My son, do not walk in the way with them. Keep your feet from their path.

(Proverbs 1:10; 15, NASB)

Watch and pray so that you will not fall into temptation. The spirit is willing, but the body is weak.

(Matthew 26:41, NIV)

No temptation has seized you except what is common to man. And God is faithful; he will not let you be tempted beyond what you can bear. But when you are tempted, he will also provide a way out so that you can stand up under it.

(1 Corinthians 10:13, NIV)

Brothers, if someone is caught in a sin, you who are spiritual should restore him gently. But watch yourself, or you also may be tempted.

(Galatians 6:1, NIV)

And do not give the devil an opportunity.

(Ephesians 4:27, NASB)

Because he himself suffered when he was tempted, he is able to help those who are being tempted.

(Hebrews 2:18, NIV)

For we do not have a high priest who cannot sympathize with our weaknesses, but One who has been tempted in all things as we are, yet without sin.

(Hebrews 4:15, NASB)

When tempted, no one should say, "God is tempting me." For God cannot be tempted by evil, nor does he tempt anyone; but each one is tempted when, by his own evil desire, he is dragged away and enticed.

(James 1:13–14, NIV)

You adulterous people, don't you know that friendship with the world is hatred toward God? Anyone who chooses to be a friend of the world becomes an enemy of God.

(James 4:4, NIV)

As obedient children, do not conform to the evil desires you had when you lived in ignorance.

(1 Peter 1:14, NIV)

And if he rescued Lot, a righteous man, who was distressed by the filthy lives of lawless men (for that righteous man, living among them day after day, was tormented in his righteous soul by the lawless deeds he saw and heard)—if this is so, then the Lord knows how to rescue godly men from trials and to hold the unrighteous for the day of judgment, while continuing their punishment. This is especially true of those who follow the corrupt desire of the sinful nature and despise authority.

(2 Peter 2:7–10a, NIV)

Terrorism
(see Fear and Violence)

Thankfulness

Enter into His gates with thanksgiving, and into His courts with praise. Be thankful to Him, and bless His name. For the Lord is good; His mercy is everlasting, and His truth endures to all generations.

(Psalm 100:4–5, NKJV)

Oh, give thanks to the Lord, for He is good! For His mercy endures forever.

(Psalm 107:1, NKJV)

Therefore as you have received Christ Jesus the Lord, so walk in Him, having been firmly rooted and now being built up in Him and established in your faith, just as you were instructed, and overflowing with gratitude.

(Colossians 2:6–7, NASB)

And whatever you do in word or deed, do all in the name of the Lord Jesus, giving thanks to God the Father through Him.

(Colossians 3:17, NKJV)

Give thanks in all circumstances, for this is God's will for you in Christ Jesus.

(1 Thessalonians 5:18, NIV)

Therefore, since we are receiving a kingdom that cannot

be shaken, let us be thankful, and so worship God acceptably with reverence and awe.

(Hebrews 12:28, NIV)

Tithing
(see Generosity and Giving)

Trouble
(see also Hardship)

Then his wife said to him, "Do you still hold fast your
integrity? Curse God and die!"

But he said to her, "You speak as one of the foolish
women speaks. Shall we indeed accept good from God
and not accept adversity?" In all this Job did not sin with
his lips.

(Job 2:9–10, NASB)

As I myself have seen, those who plow iniquity and sow
trouble and mischief reap the same.

(Job 4:8, AMP)

You, O Lord, keep my lamp burning; my God turns my
darkness into light.

(Psalm 18:28, NIV)

The troubles of my heart are multiplied; bring me out
of my distresses. Behold my affliction and my pain and
forgive all my sins [of thinking and doing].

(Psalm 25:17–18, AMP)

A righteous man may have many troubles, but the Lord delivers him from them all.

(Psalm 34:19, NIV)

You who have shown me many troubles and distresses will revive me again, and will bring me up again from the depths of the earth. May You increase my greatness and turn to comfort me.

(Psalm 71:20–21, NASB)

Even in darkness light dawns for the upright, for the gracious and compassionate and righteous man.

(Psalm 112:4, NIV)

The righteous will be remembered forever. He will not fear evil tidings; his heart is steadfast, trusting in the Lord.

(Psalm 112:6b-7, NASB)

Look upon my suffering and deliver me, for I have not forgotten your law.

(Psalm 119:153, NIV)

Though I walk in the midst of trouble, You will revive me.

(Psalm 138:7a, NKJV)

If you falter in times of trouble, how small is your strength!

(Proverbs 24:10, NIV)

Happy is the man who is always reverent, but he who hardens his heart will fall into calamity.

(Proverbs 28:14, NKJV)

And we know that in all things God works for the good of those who love him, who have been called according to his purpose. Who shall separate us from the love of Christ? Shall trouble or hardship or persecution or famine or nakedness or danger or sword?

(Romans 8:28, 35, NIV)

Let us therefore come boldly to the throne of grace, that we may obtain mercy and find grace to help in time of need.

(Hebrews 4:16, NKJV)

Is any one of you in trouble? He should pray. Is anyone happy? Let him sing songs of praise.

(James 5:13, NIV)

Trust

Our fathers trusted in You; they trusted, and You delivered them. They cried to You, and were delivered; they trusted in You, and were not ashamed.

(Psalm 22:4–5, NKJV)

Many are the sorrows of the wicked, but he who trusts in the Lord, lovingkindness shall surround him.

(Psalm 32:10, NASB)

Oh, taste and see that the Lord is good; blessed is the man who trusts in Him!

(Psalm 34:8, NKJV)

O Lord of hosts, blessed is the man who trusts in You!

(Psalm 84:12, NKJV)

Fear of man will prove to be a snare, but whoever trusts in the Lord is kept safe.

(Proverbs 29:25, NIV)

You will keep in perfect peace him whose mind is steadfast, because he trusts in you. Trust in the Lord forever, for the Lord, the Lord, is the Rock eternal.

(Isaiah 26:3–4, NIV)

Blessed is the man who trusts in the Lord, and whose hope is the Lord. For he shall be like a tree planted by the waters, which spreads out its roots by the river.

(Jeremiah 17:7–8a, NKJV)

Vengeance
(see Revenge)

Violence

The Lord tests the righteous, but the wicked and the one who loves violence His soul hates.

(Psalm 11:5, NKJV)

Do not be afraid of sudden terror, nor of trouble from the wicked when it comes; for the Lord will be your confidence, and will keep your foot from being caught.

(Proverbs 3:25–26, NKJV)

The mouth of the righteous is a fountain of life, but violence overwhelms the mouth of the wicked.

(Proverbs 10:11, NIV)

Then Jesus said to him, Put your sword back into its place, for all who draw the sword will die by the sword.

(Matthew 26:52, AMP)

What is the source of quarrels and conflicts among you? Is not the source your pleasures that wage war in your members? You lust and do not have; so you commit murder. You are envious and cannot obtain; so you fight and quarrel. You do not have because you do not ask. You ask and do not receive, because you ask with wrong motives, so that you may spend it on your pleasures. You adulteresses, do you not know that friendship with the world is hostility toward God? Therefore whoever wishes to be a friend of the world makes himself an enemy of God.

(James 4:1–4, NASB)

Weight Control

It is not good to eat too much honey. Like a city whose walls are broken down is a man who lacks self-control.

(Proverbs 25:27a, 28, NIV)

Please test your servants for ten days: Give us nothing but vegetables to eat and water to drink. Then compare our appearance with that of the young men who eat the royal food, and treat your servants in accordance with what you see. So he agreed to this and tested them for ten days. At the end of the ten days they looked healthier and better nourished than any of the young men who ate the royal food.

(Daniel 1:12–15, NIV)

The spirit is willing, but the body is weak.

(Matthew 26:41b, NIV)

"Everything is permissible"—but not everything is beneficial. "Everything is permissible"—but not everything is constructive.

(1 Corinthians 10:23, NIV)

Will of God

The Lord will fulfill his purpose for me.

(Psalm 138:8a, NIV)

Your kingdom come. Your will be done on earth as it is in heaven.

(Matthew 6:10, NKJV)

For whoever does the will of My Father in heaven is My brother and sister and mother.

(Matthew 12:50, NKJV)

We know that God does not listen to sinners. He listens to the godly man who does his will.

(John 9:31, NIV)

From one man he made every nation of men, that they should inhabit the whole earth; and he determined the times set for them and the exact places where they should live.

(Acts 17:26, NIV)

Do not conform any longer to the pattern of this world, but be transformed by the renewing of your mind. Then you will be able to test and approve what God's will is—his good, pleasing and perfect will.

(Romans 12:2, NIV)

In him we were also chosen, having been predestined according to the plan of him who works out everything in conformity with the purpose of his will.

(Ephesians 1:11, NIV)

For it is God who is at work in you, both to will and to work for His good pleasure.

(Philippians 2:13, NASB)

Be joyful always; pray continually; give thanks in all circumstances, for this is God's will for you in Christ Jesus.

(1 Thessalonians 5:16–18, NIV)

So do not throw away your confidence; it will be richly rewarded. You need to persevere so that when you have done the will of God, you will receive what he has promised.

(Hebrews 10:35–36, NIV)

As a result, he does not live the rest of his earthly life for evil human desires, but rather for the will of God.

(1 Peter 4:2, NIV)

The world and its desires pass away, but the man who does the will of God lives forever.

(1 John 2:17, NIV)

Wisdom

The law of the Lord is perfect, restoring the soul; the testimony of the Lord is sure, making wise the simple.

(Psalm 19:7, NASB)

The fear of the Lord is the beginning of knowledge, but fools despise wisdom and instruction.

(Proverbs 1:7, NKJV)

Yes, if you cry out for insight and raise your voice for understanding, if you seek [Wisdom] as for silver and search for skillful and godly Wisdom as for hidden treasures, then you will understand the reverent and worshipful fear of the Lord and find the knowledge of [our omniscient] God. For the Lord gives skillful and godly Wisdom; from His mouth come knowledge and understanding.

(Proverbs 2:3–6, AMP)

Acquire wisdom! Acquire understanding! Do not forget nor turn away from the words of my mouth. Do not forsake her, and she will guard you; love her, and she will watch over you. The beginning of wisdom is: Acquire wisdom; and with all your acquiring, get understanding.

(Proverbs 4:5–7, NASB)

A fool finds pleasure in evil conduct, but a man of understanding delights in wisdom.

(Proverbs 10:23, NIV)

A man is praised according to his wisdom, but men with warped minds are despised.

(Proverbs 12:8, NIV)

He who walks with wise men will be wise, but the companion of fools will suffer harm.

(Proverbs 13:20, NASB)

He who gets wisdom loves his own soul; he who cherishes understanding prospers.

(Proverbs 19:8, NIV)

A man's wisdom gives him patience; it is to his glory to overlook an offense.

(Proverbs 19:11, NIV)

There is gold, and an abundance of jewels; but the lips of knowledge are a more precious thing.

(Proverbs 20:15, NASB)

There is no [human] wisdom or understanding or counsel [that can prevail] against the Lord.

(Proverbs 21:30, Amp)

Know also that wisdom is sweet to your soul; if you find
it, there is a future hope for you, and your hope will not
be cut off.

(Proverbs 24:14, niv)

For to the person who pleases Him God gives wisdom
and knowledge and joy.

(Ecclesiastes 2:26a, Amp)

Therefore whoever hears these sayings of Mine, and does
them, I will liken him to a wise man who built his house
on the rock: and the rain descended, the floods came, and
the winds blew and beat on that house; and it did not fall,
for it was founded on the rock.

(Matthew 7:24–25, nkjv)

For the foolishness of God is wiser than man's wisdom, and the weakness of God is stronger than man's
strength.

(1 Corinthians 1:25, niv)

Let no man deceive himself. If any man among you thinks
that he is wise in this age, he must become foolish, so that
he may become wise. For the wisdom of this world is
foolishness before God.

(1 Corinthians 3:18–19a, nasb)

Therefore be careful how you walk, not as unwise men but as wise, making the most of your time, because the days are evil.

(Ephesians 5:15–16, NASB)

If any of you lacks wisdom, he should ask God, who gives generously to all without finding fault, and it will be given to him.

(James 1:5, NIV)

Who is wise and understanding among you? Let him show it by his good life, by deeds done in the humility that comes from wisdom.

(James 3:13, NIV)

But the wisdom that comes from heaven is first of all pure; then peace-loving, considerate, submissive, full of mercy and good fruit, impartial and sincere.

(James 3:17, NIV)

Witnessing
(see also Character)

I will praise you forever for what you have done; in your name I will hope, for your name is good. I will praise you in the presence of your saints.

(Psalm 52:9, NIV)

Come and hear, all you who reverently and worshipfully fear God, and I will declare what He has done for me!

(Psalm 66:16, AMP)

The fruit of the righteous is a tree of life, and he who wins souls is wise.

(Proverbs 11:30, NKJV)

Listen (consent and submit) to the words of the wise, and apply your mind to my knowledge; for it will be pleasant if you keep them in your mind [believing them]; your lips will be accustomed to [confessing] them.

(Proverbs 22:17–18, AMP)

Hear me, you who know what is right, you people who have my law in your hearts: Do not fear the reproach of men or be terrified by their insults.

(Isaiah 51:7, NIV)

Blessed are you when people insult you and persecute you, and falsely say all kinds of evil against you because of Me. Rejoice and be glad, for your reward in heaven is great; for in the same way they persecuted the prophets who were before you.

(Matthew 5:11–12, NASB)

You are the light of the world. A city set on a hill cannot be hidden; nor does anyone light a lamp and put it under a basket, but on the lampstand, and it gives light to all who are in the house. Let your light shine before men in such a way that they may see your good works, and glorify your Father who is in heaven.

(Matthew 5:14–16, NASB)

Therefore whoever confesses Me before men, him I will also confess before My Father who is in heaven. But whoever denies Me before men, him I will also deny before My Father who is in heaven.

(Matthew 10:32–33, NKJV)

Go therefore and make disciples of all the nations, baptizing them in the name of the Father and of the Son and of the Holy Spirit, teaching them to observe all things that I have commanded you; and lo, I am with you always, even to the end of the age.

(Matthew 28:19–20, NKJV)

For whoever is ashamed of Me and My words in this adulterous and sinful generation, of him the Son of Man also will be ashamed when He comes in the glory of His Father with the holy angels.

(Mark 8:38, NKJV)

And He said to them, "Go into all the world and preach the gospel to all creation."

(Mark 16:15, NASB)

He who is not with Me is against Me, and he who does not gather with Me scatters.

(Luke 11:23, NKJV)

Also I say to you, whoever confesses Me before men, him the Son of Man also will confess before the angels of God. But he who denies Me before men will be denied before the angels of God.

(Luke 12:8–9, NKJV)

For I am not ashamed of the gospel, for it is the power of God for salvation to everyone who believes.

(Romans 1:16a, NASB)

How then shall they call on Him in whom they have not believed? And how shall they believe in Him of whom they have not heard? And how shall they hear without a preacher?

(Romans 10:14, NKJV)

It is good neither to eat meat nor drink wine nor do anything by which your brother stumbles or is offended or is made weak.

(Romans 14:21, NKJV)

To the weak I became weak, that I might win the weak; I have become all things to all men, so that I may by all means save some.

(1 Corinthians 9:22, NASB)

So whether you eat or drink or whatever you do, do it all for the glory of God. Do not cause anyone to stumble, whether Jews, Greeks or the church of God—even as I try to please everybody in every way. For I am not seeking my own good but the good of many, so that they may be saved.

(1 Corinthians 10:31–33, NIV)

Unlike so many, we do not peddle the word of God for profit. On the contrary, in Christ we speak before God with sincerity, like men sent from God.

(2 Corinthians 2:17, NIV)

And since we have the same spirit of faith, according to what is written, "I believed and therefore I spoke," we also believe and therefore speak.

(2 Corinthians 4:13, NKJV)

Therefore, we are ambassadors for Christ, as though God were making an appeal through us.

(2 Corinthians 5:20a, NASB)

For we take thought beforehand and aim to be honest and absolutely above suspicion, not only in the sight of the Lord but also in the sight of men.

(2 Corinthians 8:21, AMP)

Because of the service by which you have proved yourselves, men will praise God for the obedience that accompanies your confession of the gospel of Christ, and for your generosity in sharing with them and with everyone else.

(2 Corinthians 9:13, NIV)

Let us not become weary in doing good, for at the proper time we will reap a harvest if we do not give up. Therefore, as we have opportunity, let us do good to all people, especially to those who belong to the family of believers.

(Galatians 6:9–10, NIV)

Do everything without complaining or arguing, so that you may become blameless and pure, children of God without fault in a crooked and depraved generation, in which you shine like stars in the universe.

(Philippians 2:14–15, NIV)

Let your gentleness be known to all men. The Lord is at hand.

(Philippians 4:5, NKJV)

Let your conversation be always full of grace, seasoned with salt, so that you may know how to answer everyone.

(Colossians 4:6, NIV)

Don't let anyone look down on you because you are young, but set an example for the believers in speech, in life, in love, in faith and in purity.

(1 Timothy 4:12, NIV)

So do not be ashamed to testify about our Lord.

(2 Timothy 1:8a, NIV)

Similarly, encourage the young men to be self-controlled. In everything set them an example by doing what is good. In your teaching show integrity, seriousness and soundness of speech that cannot be condemned, so that those who oppose you may be ashamed because they have nothing bad to say about us.

(Titus 2:6–8, NIV)

I pray that you may be active in sharing your faith, so that you will have a full understanding of every good thing we have in Christ.

(Philemon 6, NIV)

Live such good lives among the pagans that, though they

accuse you of doing wrong, they may see your good deeds and glorify God on the day he visits us.

(1 Peter 2:12, NIV)

But in your hearts set Christ apart as holy [and acknowledge Him] as Lord. Always be ready to give a logical defense to anyone who asks you to account for the hope that is in you, but do it courteously and respectfully. [And see to it that] your conscience is entirely clear (unimpaired), so that, when you are falsely accused as evildoers, those who threaten you abusively and revile your right behavior in Christ may come to be ashamed [of slandering your good lives].

(1 Peter 3:15–16, AMP)

If anyone speaks, he should do it as one speaking the very words of God. If anyone serves, he should do it with the strength God provides, so that in all things God may be praised through Jesus Christ. To him be the glory and the power for ever and ever. Amen.

(1 Peter 4:11, NIV)

If you are reviled for the name of Christ, you are blessed, because the Spirit of glory and of God rests on you. Make sure that none of you suffers as a murderer, or thief, or evildoer, or a troublesome meddler; but if anyone suffers as a Christian, he is not to be ashamed, but is to glorify God in this name.

(1 Peter 4:14–16, NASB)

Be merciful to those who doubt; snatch others from the fire and save them; to others show mercy, mixed with fear—hating even the clothing stained by corrupted flesh.

(Jude 22–23, NIV)

Word of God

So He humbled you, allowed you to hunger, and fed you with manna which you did not know nor did your fathers know, that He might make you know that man shall not live by bread alone; but man lives by every word that proceeds from the mouth of the Lord.

(Deuteronomy 8:3, NKJV)

I have not departed from the commandment of His lips; I have treasured the words of His mouth more than my necessary food.

(Job 23:12, NKJV)

Your word have I laid up in my heart, that I might not sin against You.

(Psalm 119:11, AMP)

I rejoice in following your statutes as one rejoices in great riches. I meditate on your precepts and consider your ways. I delight in your decrees; I will not neglect your word.

(Psalm 119:14–16, NIV)

Your word is a lamp to my feet and a light to my path.

(Psalm 119:105, NKJV)

All your words are true; all your righteous laws are eternal.

(Psalm 119:160, NIV)

Every word of God is tested; He is a shield to those who take refuge in Him. Do not add to His words or He will reprove you, and you will be proved a liar.

(Proverbs 30:5–6, NASB)

The grass withers, the flower fades, but the word of our God stands forever.

(Isaiah 40:8, NKJV)

For as the rain comes down, and the snow from heaven, and do not return there, but water the earth, and make it bring forth and bud, that it may give seed to the sower and bread to the eater, so shall My word be that goes forth from My mouth; it shall not return to Me void, but it shall accomplish what I please, and it shall prosper in the thing for which I sent it.

(Isaiah 55:10–11, NKJV)

Do not think that I came to abolish the Law or the Prophets; I did not come to abolish but to fulfill. For truly I say to you, until heaven and earth pass away, not the smallest letter or stroke shall pass from the Law until all is accomplished.

(Matthew 5:17–18, NASB)

But Jesus replied to them, You are wrong because you know neither the Scriptures nor God's power.

(Matthew 22:29, Amp)

Heaven and earth will pass away, but My words will by no means pass away.

(Matthew 24:35, nkjv)

While Jesus was saying these things, one of the women in the crowd raised her voice and said to Him, "Blessed is the womb that bore You and the breasts at which You nursed."

But He said, "On the contrary, blessed are those who hear the word of God and observe it."

(Luke 11:27–28, nasb)

For everything that was written in the past was written to teach us, so that through endurance and the encouragement of the Scriptures we might have hope.

(Romans 15:4, niv)

For I want you to know, brethren, that the Gospel which was proclaimed and made known by me is not man's gospel [a human invention, according to or patterned after any human standard]. For indeed I did not receive it from man, nor was I taught it, but [it came to me] through a [direct] revelation [given] by Jesus Christ (the Messiah).

(Galatians 1:11–12, Amp)

For this reason we also constantly thank God that when you received the word of God which you heard from us, you accepted it not as the word of men, but for what it really is, the word of God, which also performs its work in you who believe.

(1 Thessalonians 2:13, NASB)

All Scripture is inspired by God and profitable for teaching, for reproof, for correction, for training in righteousness; so that the man of God may be adequate, equipped for every good work.

(2 Timothy 3:16–17, NASB)

For the word of God is living and active. It judges the thoughts and attitudes of the heart.

(Hebrews 4:12a,c, NIV)

I testify to everyone who hears the words of the prophecy of this book: if anyone adds to them, God will add to him the plagues which are written in this book; and if anyone takes away from the words of the book of this prophecy, God will take away his part from the tree of life and from the holy city, which are written in this book.

(Revelation 22:18–19, NASB)

Working
(see also Business)

He who works his land will have abundant food, but he who chases fantasies lacks judgment.

(Proverbs 12:11, NIV)

In all labor there is profit, but idle talk leads only to poverty.

(Proverbs 14:23, Amp)

A worker's appetite works for him, for his hunger urges him on.

(Proverbs 16:26, nasb)

He who is loose and slack in his work is brother to him who is a destroyer and he who does not use his endeavors to heal himself is brother to him who commits suicide.

(Proverbs 18:9, Amp)

What does the worker gain from his toil? I have seen the burden God has laid on men. I know that there is nothing better for men than to be happy and do good while they live. That everyone may eat and drink, and find satisfaction in all his toil—this is the gift of God.

(Ecclesiastes 3:9–10; 12–13, niv)

So I saw that there is nothing better for a man than to enjoy his work, because that is his lot.

(Ecclesiastes 3: 22a, niv)

Moreover, when God gives any man wealth and possessions, and enables him to enjoy them, to accept his lot and be happy in his work—this is a gift of God.

(Ecclesiastes 5:19, niv)

Whatever your hand finds to do, do it with all your might, for in the grave, where you are going, there is neither working nor planning nor knowledge nor wisdom.

(Ecclesiastes 9:10, NIV)

Now to a laborer, his wages are not counted as a favor or a gift, but as an obligation (something owed to him).

(Romans 4:4, AMP)

So then neither the one who plants nor the one who waters is anything, but God who causes the growth. Now he who plants and he who waters are one; but each will receive his own reward according to his own labor.

(1 Corinthians 3:7–8, NASB)

Whatever may be your task, work at it heartily (from the soul), as [something done] for the Lord and not for men.

(Colossians 3:23, AMP)

Make it your ambition to lead a quiet life, to mind your own business and to work with your hands, just as we told you, so that your daily life may win the respect of outsiders and so that you will not be dependent on anybody.

(1 Thessalonians 4:11–12, NIV)

Worry
(see Depression and Sorrow)

Worship

Oh come, let us worship and bow down; let us kneel before the Lord our Maker. For He is our God, and we are the people of His pasture, and the sheep of His hand.

(Psalm 95:6–7a, NKJV)

Oh, worship the Lord in the beauty of holiness!

(Psalm 96:9a, NKJV)

The Lord says: "These people come near to me with their mouth and honor me with their lips, but their hearts are far from me. Their worship of me is made up only of rules taught by men."

(Isaiah 29:13, NIV)

But the hour is coming, and now is, when the true worshipers will worship the Father in spirit and truth; for the Father is seeking such to worship Him. God is Spirit, and those who worship Him must worship in spirit and truth.

(John 4:23–24, NKJV)

Therefore, I urge you, brothers, in view of God's mercy, to offer your bodies as living sacrifices, holy and pleasing to God—this is your spiritual act of worship.

(Romans 12:1, NIV)

Therefore, since we are receiving a kingdom that cannot be shaken, let us be thankful, and so worship God acceptably with reverence and awe.

(Hebrews 12:28, NIV)

Youth, Expectations of

Regard (treat with honor, due obedience, and courtesy) your father and mother, that your days may be long in the land the Lord your God gives you.

(Exodus 20:12, AMP)

Cursed is he who dishonors his father or his mother.

(Deuteronomy 27:16a, AMP)

My son, keep your father's commands and do not forsake your mother's teaching. Bind them upon your heart forever; fasten them around your neck. When you walk, they will guide you; when you sleep, they will watch over you; when you awake, they will speak to you. For these commands are a lamp, this teaching is a light, and the corrections of discipline are the way to life.

(Proverbs 6:20–23, NIV)

A wise son makes a father glad, but a foolish son is a grief to his mother.

(Proverbs 10:1, NASB)

A fool rejects his father's discipline, but he who regards reproof is sensible.

(Proverbs 15:5, NASB)

Even a child is known by his acts, whether [or not] what he does is pure and right.

(Proverbs 20:11, AMP)

Listen to your father, who gave you life, and do not despise your mother when she is old.

(Proverbs 23:22, NIV)

Rejoice, young man, during your childhood, and let your heart be pleasant during the days of young manhood. And follow the impulses of your heart and the desires of your eyes. Yet know that God will bring you to judgment for all these things.

(Ecclesiastes 11:9, NASB)

Remember now your Creator in the days of your youth, before the difficult days come, and the years draw near when you say, "I have no pleasure in them."

(Ecclesiastes 12:1, NKJV)

You know the commandments: "Do not commit adultery," "Do not murder," "Do not steal," "Do not bear false witness," "Honor your father and your mother."

(Luke 18:20, NKJV)

Children, obey your parents in the Lord, for this is right. "Honor your father and mother," which is the first commandment with promise: "that it may be well with you and you may live long on the earth."

(Ephesians 6:1–3, NKJV)

Children, obey your parents in all things, for this is well pleasing to the Lord.

(Colossians 3:20, NKJV)

Flee the evil desires of youth, and pursue righteousness, faith, love and peace, along with those who call on the Lord out of a pure heart.

(2 Timothy 2:22, NIV)